MODERNITY
AND THE
ARCHITECTURE
OF MEXICO

MODERNITY AND THE ARCHITECTURE OF MEXICO

Editor

Edward R. Burian

University of Texas Press, Austin

. . . para mis amigas y amigos mexicanos . . .
y el "contingente latino" . . .

Requests for permission to reproduce material from this work should be sent to
Permissions, University of Texas Press, Box 7819, Austin, TX 78713-7819.

∞ The paper used in this publication meets the minimum requirements of American
National Standard for Information Sciences—Permanence of Paper for Printed
Library Materials, ANSI Z39.48-1984.

LIBRARY OF CONGRESS CATALOGING-IN-PUBLICATION DATA

Burian, Edward R., 1953–
    Modernity and the architecture of Mexico / Edward R. Burian.—1st University
of Texas Press ed.
        p.   cm.
    Includes bibliographical references and index.
    ISBN 0-292-70853-X (paper : alk. paper)

    1. Architecture, Modern—20th century—Mexico.   2. Architecture—Mexico.
    1. Title.
NA755.B87   1997
720'.972—dc20
                                                            96-27584

CONTENTS

vii Foreword by Ricardo Legorreta

ix Acknowledgments

3 Introduction

13 *Alberto Pérez-Gómez*
MEXICO, MODERNITY, AND ARCHITECTURE
An Interview with Alberto Pérez-Gómez

61 *Antonio E. Méndez-Vigatá*
POLITICS AND ARCHITECTURAL LANGUAGE
Post-Revolutionary Regimes in Mexico and Their Influence
on Mexican Public Architecture, 1920–1952

91 *Celia Ester Arredondo Zambrano*
MODERNITY IN MEXICO: The Case of the Ciudad Universitaria

107 *Alberto Kalach*
ARCHITECTURE AND PLACE: The Stadium of the University City

115 *William J. R. Curtis*
"THE GENERAL AND THE LOCAL": Enrique del Moral's Own
House, Calle Francisco Ramírez 5, Mexico City, 1948

127 *Edward R. Burian*
THE ARCHITECTURE OF JUAN O'GORMAN: Dichotomy and Drift

151 *Carlos G. Mijares Bracho*
THE ARCHITECTURE OF CARLOS OBREGÓN SANTACILIA
A Work for Its Time and Context

163 *Antonio Toca Fernández*
JUAN SEGURA: The Origins of Modern Architecture in Mexico

177 *Louise Noelle Merles*
THE ARCHITECTURE AND URBANISM OF MARIO PANI
Creativity and Compromise

191 Postscript

195 Notes on the Contributors

199 Selected Bibliography

213 Index

FOREWORD

Much has been written and discussed in recent years concerning the relationship of modernity to architecture. In this regard, it is very difficult to precisely understand the concept of modernity in a country such as Mexico, where apparent opposites converge . . . rootedness and innovation, the ancient and the contemporary, romanticism and pragmatism as well as gentleness and strength. In Mexico, there is little possibility of understanding these dichotomies of our culture without both living in and loving our country, as many significant aspects of our history and character do not have a rational explanation. In this context, the architects active between the 1920s and 1960s were proudly Mexican, and typify this paradigm in terms of their professional posture and built work.

This generation of architects truly understood culture, which was devoted to the service of society and the profession. They are an example of the role that the architect ought to play in society.

In a time when egocentrism and commercialization dominate the architectural world, it is very healthy to study the work of a group of architects that bravely looked to their native roots in undertaking the task of the modernization of the country. This was characterized by truly robust form making by a talented generation of Mexican architects who made a valuable contribution to the development of world architecture without losing their individual characteristics. Unfortunately, because of the centralized control of the architectural media, as well as the humility of these architects, their work did not become well known or particularly valued around the world.

This excellent study by Edward Burian presents architects, individual works, and concepts of surprising quality and also raises important questions. This book is, without a doubt, of great value for professionals and students to reevaluate an architecture of great maturity and objectivity, which is, unfortunately, uncommon in our times.

Ricardo Legorreta
Mexico City, July 1995

ACKNOWLEDGMENTS

I would like to thank the following institutions and individuals who made the publication of this book possible. Without their support this book would not have come to fruition.

I initially investigated the architecture of Mexico during my graduate studies at the Yale School of Architecture, where I was given the opportunity to pursue my interests in the supportive and open-minded atmosphere of the school. I owe a debt of gratitude to Professors Tom Beeby, Alan Plattus, Patrick Pinnell, and George Ranalli from the Yale School of Architecture as well as to Professors George Kubler, Mary Miller, and Vincent Scully from the Yale Department of the History of Art.

The Department of Architecture at Texas A&M assisted me in the preparation of this manuscript. Julius Gribou, Head of the Department, lent his support for my undertaking of this project. Rechelle Parker, Angela Owen, and Glenda Draper were extraordinarily helpful in the production of the book. Angela Owen diligently transcribed my interview with Alberto Pérez-Gómez, while Glenda Draper meticulously typed several of the essays that were translated from Spanish.

I was able to focus my thoughts on the architecture of modern Mexico while teaching a seminar on the Art and Architecture of Twentieth-Century Mexico during the spring semesters of 1992–1994. Special thanks should also be extended to the staff at the Benson Latin American Collection at the University of Texas at Austin and to the librarians at the Harvard Graduate School of Design, who were helpful in assisting me with my research for this book.

The former Director of the School of Architecture at the Instituto Tecnológico y de Estudios Superiores de Monterrey (ITESM), Arq. Antonio Méndez-Vigatá, was extraordinarily hospitable during my visits to Mexico City and helped me develop many of my thoughts concerning Mexican architecture. He provided numerous insights into the subtleties of the architectural culture and intellectual history of Mexico, from the inception of the book through its completion. Professor Celia Arredondo graciously showed me the work of Enrique de la Mora in Monterrey. Arq. Vladimir Kaspé, a major protagonist in the early Modern architecture of Mexico, graciously invited me to his home and studio and shared his personal memories of Mario Pani and the decades of the thirties, forties, and fifties in Mexico. Enrique Norten was an early supporter of this project and generously showed me through his office during a visit to Mexico City. Patrick Pinnell of the Yale School of Architecture and Xavier Cortés Rocha and Luis Arnal Simón of the Universidad Nacional Autónoma de México (UNAM) School of Architecture lent their encouragement during the formative stages of this project. Larry Speck, Dean of the School of Architecture at the University of Texas at Austin, was an enthusiastic supporter of the project. As the book neared completion, Ricardo Legorreta provided his encouragement and shared his memories of a generation of Mexican architects who preceded him. I am grateful to him for generously agreeing to write the foreword to the book. Idalia Toledo offered many insights into the poetic aspects of Mexican culture. José Carlos Fernández assisted me in contacting several architectural scholars in Mexico and with the translation of several essays that appear in this volume. Roberto Rodríguez also helped translate several essays that appear in this book. I am particularly grateful to him for patiently explaining the Mexican nuances of many phrases in Spanish. Bertha Olmos shared her firsthand experiences regarding the complexity, drama, and humor of Mexican life as well as her broad range of interests in Mexican architecture and culture.

My colleagues in Los Angeles, Janek Bielski and Janek Tabencki, have offered continuous support through the years for my interest and enthusiasm for the art and architecture of Mexico. Joseph McFaul lent his lucid advice on many aspects of the book as it went into production. Scott Wood and Greg Gross continue to be sounding boards for many of my observations on the culture of Mexico.

Louise Noelle Merles generously assisted me in obtaining many of the photographs that are reproduced in this volume. Her prompt responses and enthusiasm for this project were invaluable in making this book a reality. Elena Abrahamsson took many of the original photographs that appear in this book during a trip to Mexico City in March of 1995. Antonio Toca helped me photograph the work of Juan Segura during a trip to Mexico City in June of 1995.

Elena Abrahamsson and Lilia Gonzales translated several articles on the functional architecture of the 1930s in Mexico and addresses by Juan O'Gorman that provided an intellectual context for my essay. Steven Moore, who read an early version of my essay, was unfailingly helpful in providing criticism and insights into the dichotomies of the work of Juan O'Gorman, and has influenced much of my thinking in relation to the issues of technology, representation, and place. He also read the introduction and postscript to this book as well as Antonio Méndez-Vigatá's essay and made many lucid comments, characteristically drawing upon the broad range of tools in his critical arsenal.

The staff at the University of Texas Press were unfailingly helpful in the production of this book. Theresa May, Lois Rankin, Heidi Haeuser, and Nancy Warrington each made special contributions in seeing this book come to realization.

Special mention and thanks must be extended to each of the contributors who industriously researched and wrote the essays featured in this book. Without their devotion to the cause of Mexican architecture, this project would not have been possible.

Finally, I would like to thank the people of Mexico, who shared their art and architecture with me. They patiently answered my questions, allowed me access to their architecture, and provided innumerable insights into their magnificent culture.

Edward R. Burian
Tucson

MODERNITY

AND THE

ARCHITECTURE

OF MEXICO

INTRODUCTION

The title of this book suggests a critical[1] discussion of the notion of modernity and its unique development within Mexican architecture and urbanism from the period of political stabilization that began in 1928 after the Mexican Revolution to the social and political upheaval associated with the Olympic Games in Mexico City in 1968. While revolutions and games are not bookends, in this case they serve as useful demarcations of architectural activity in Mexico.

The publication of this book at this time is particularly appropriate given the current state of architectural culture in both the United States and Mexico. Since the mid-1970s there has been an extraordinary renewed interest in early Modern architecture (at least in terms of form and imagery, if not ideology), both as a way of gaining insight into current architectural culture and as a reaction to the recent phenomenon of neoconservative post-Modernism. The repercussions of this phenomenon have been felt in schools of architecture and in the profession at large. Spurred on by the interests of a generation of architects in North America and Europe, a vast array of books and commentaries have appeared on the architectural scene. In Mexico, the projects of a younger generation of architects have focused renewed attention on the roots of Modern architecture in their country.

The ever more closely intertwined relationship between the United States and Mexico provides a backdrop for this book. In the American Southwest, there is an increased blurring of the border between the two countries in terms of population, economics, and culture. With the recent signing of the NAFTA trade agreements, architects from the United States are looking to Mexico not only in economic terms as a market for their architectural services, but also in broader cultural terms for both insight and inspiration to create a meaningful architecture that engages the issue of place, and more specifically, an architecture appropriate for the conditions of the American Southwest.

While my initial interest in this powerful body of work was from the point of view of a practicing architect from Los Angeles, and was primarily visual and formal, I also desired to understand this work in more critical terms. Thus, this book is a way of understanding this work by examining underlying ideas, ideological and political constructs, and specific architects' agendas for my own personal insight and also for the opportunity to represent this work to a broader audience that barely knows of its existence.

In this context, the intention of this book is to focus on a group of early Modern twentieth-century Mexican architects, and their buildings, projects, and manifestos, that have largely been ignored in architectural literature, particularly in English. Although one cannot ignore the work of such well-known Mexican architects as Luis Barragán, Ricardo Legorreta, Carlos Mijares, Pedro Ramírez Vázquez, Teodoro González de León, Agustín Hernández, and Abraham Zabludovsky, their work is relatively well published in a variety of monographs.[2] My goal is instead to selectively reexamine a generation of early Moderns in Mexico whose works of architecture, projects, and manifestos have largely been jettisoned by history and who are representative of the best work of the period. This early group of moderns includes the following architects, whom I have subdivided by approximate generation in descending order for greater clarity. Even a cursory glance at this list reveals how thoroughly these architects and their work have been forgotten.

Manuel Ortiz Monasterio (1887–1967)

Carlos Obregón Santacilia (1896–1961)

Juan Segura (1898–1989)

Vicente Mendiola (1900–1986)

José Villagrán García (1901–1982)

Juan Legarreta (1902–1934)

Francisco Serrano (1900–1982)

Max Cetto (1903–1980)

Juan O'Gorman (1905–1982)

Ignacio Díaz Morales (1905–1992)

Enrique del Moral (1906–1987)

Enrique Aragón Echeagaray (1906–)

Enrique de la Mora y Palomar (1907–1978)

José Gorbea Trueba (1907–)

Enrique Yáñez (1908–1990)

Augusto Pérez Palacios (1909–)

Vladimir Kaspé (1910–)

Mario Pani (1911–1993)

Augusto Alvarez (1914–1995)

Juan Sordo Madaleno (1916–1985)

Enrique Landa (1921–)

Víctor de la Lama (1919–)

Ramón Torres (1924–)

Héctor Velázquez (1923–)

Jorge González Reyna (1929–1969)

0.1. Juan Sordo Madaleno, Seguros Anahuac (Anahuac Insurance Building), Mexico City, 1957–1958. Photo by Edward R. Burian.

0.2. Enrique del Moral, Enrique Ortiz, and Francisco López García, office building at the corner of Insurgentes and Londres, Mexico City, 1950. Photo by Edward R. Burian.

0.3. Manuel Ortiz Monasterio, La Compañía Nacional de Seguros (The National Insurance Company Building), Mexico City, 1930–1932. Photo by Edward R. Burian.

0.4. Francisco J. Serrano, "Cine Encanto" movie theater, Mexico City, late 1930s. Photo courtesy of the Archive of Louise Noelle Merles.

0.5. José Villagrán García, Villagrán García Residence, Mexico City, early 1930s. Photo courtesy of the INBA, Dirección de Arquitectura.

While these architects and others could not all be discussed with specific essays in this particular volume, it is hoped that the task of reintroducing this work to an English-speaking audience will be continued by other scholars. Only the limitations of time and space prevented me from including several key figures in separate essays. Obvious omissions include Hannes Meyer and his impact on planning theory and urban design in post-Revolutionary Mexico, as well as the extraordinary architecture of Enrique de la Mora and Vladimir Kaspé, among others. However, these architects and others are reexamined more generally within the context of broader critical discussions in this volume. The architects and projects discussed in separate essays were selected on the basis of the degree to which they have been edited from history, their unique and critical contribution to the development of early Modern architecture in Mexico, as well as the individual interests of the authors who were invited to participate in this project.

Relatively little has been published in English regarding this era of Mexican architecture, and virtually nothing in terms of critical commentary. Previous studies in English have primarily been visual chronologies of individual buildings. The limited commentary that does appear tends to support the notion that Modern architecture was vaguely an extension of pre-Columbian grandeur—a way for Mexico to take her rightful place among the world's progressive, modern nations—and had the ability to remake society and solve Mexico's social problems. In this context, this book attempts to fill a gap in our critical understanding of this era of the architecture of Mexico.

Mexican architects are not even featured in Henry Russell Hitchcock and Phillip Johnson's *The International Style: Architecture Since 1922*, published in 1932. This body of work first became widely known to an English-speaking audience with the publication of Esther Born's *The New Architecture in Mexico*, in 1937, followed by I. E. Myers's *Mexico's Modern Architecture* in 1952. The catalog from the show "4000 Years of Architecture in Mexico," initiated by the Instituto Nacional de Bellas Artes (INBA; National Institute of Fine Arts) Department of Architecture and the Secretaría de Educación Pública (SEP; Ministry of Public Education), was published in 1956. Max Cetto's book *Modern Architecture in Mexico* appeared in 1961, while C. B. Smith's *Builders in the Sun* was published in 1967. Various books have since been published featuring the work of individual Mexican architects; however, the books mentioned above form the core of works written in English that contribute to our general understanding and conception of the architecture of Mexico during this period.[3]

A brief survey of the literature in Spanish is more extensive, although hardly monolithic. However, even a cursory review reveals a broader discussion in relationship to issues of politics and ideology. Issues of social responsibility, response to contemporary programs, and the fulfillment of the aspirations of the Mexican Revolution, among others, are more fully engaged. Antonio Toca's *Arquitectura contemporánea en México* appeared in 1989, while *México: Nueva arquitectura,* written with Aníbal Figueroa, was published in 1991. Pablo Quintero's *Modernidad en la arquitectura mexicana* and Rafael López Rangel's *La modernidad arquitectónica mexicana* were published in 1990 and 1989, respectively. Louise Noelle's *Catálogo guía de arquitectura contemporánea, Ciudad de México* was published in 1993, while her *Arquitectos contemporáneos de México* appeared in 1989. L. Hernández's *Análisis crítico de la arquitectura moderna en México* appeared in 1965. Israel Katzman's excellent book *La arquitectura contemporánea mexicana* surfaced in 1963. José Villagrán García himself wrote *Panorama de 50 años de arquitectura mexicana contemporánea,* while Carlos Obregón Santacilia produced *50 años de arquitectura mexicana,* both published in 1952.

The essays in this volume intentionally span a range of issues, from broad-based critical commentaries to discussions of individual architects and buildings, in order to examine modernity both as an ideological issue as well as in relationship to specific works of architecture and their individual qualities. They are presented not as a monolithic survey of the period, but rather as a gathering of scholars and interested observers with differing approaches and voices.

My interview with Alberto Pérez-Gómez provides an introduction and a broad conceptual setting for the essays that follow. Pérez-Gómez discusses the ideological background of the notion of modernity in México. He offers insights into the work and theory of individual architects such as Hannes Meyer, Félix Candela, Enrique de la Mora, and José Villagrán García. He also explores the topics of labor, mass production, nationalism, culture, and modernity itself, among others.

Antonio Méndez-Vigatá makes explicit the role of politics in post-Revolutionary Mexico from 1920 to 1952 in the formulation of architectural language and ideology, and in the forging of a national identity. The powerful role of the Ministry of Education as a formulator and disseminator of ideology and the specific role of Villagrán García as a theoretician are also discussed.

Individual projects are the focus of the next two essays. In her essay, Celia Arredondo discusses the Ciudad Universitaria (CU; University City) as an icon of Modern architecture in Mexico and explores its relationship to the conception of the universal man of the Modern movement versus the conception of a new Mexican man born out of the Mexican Revolution. Alberto Kalach examines the extraordinary stadium that is adjacent to the Ciudad Universitaria. The stadium is discussed in terms of the particular qualities of place—including the site's geology, topography, and history—in relationship to its making and tectonic order.

Discussions of individual architects whose work is largely unknown outside of Mexico round out the book. William Curtis analyzes the form and sequence of Enrique del Moral's residence including its materials and ideas as well as the issues of "the local" and the "universal." My essay on Juan O'Gorman reexamines the work of this complex architect and artist as a manifestation of juxtaposed dichotomies. O'Gorman's transition from "rational" functionalist to "irrational" organicist is redescribed as a bi-directional phenomenon over time, rather than a drastic and paradoxical conversion. Carlos Mijares traces the career of Carlos Obregón Santacilia and the interrelationship of his individual buildings to culture, place, urban sequence, and the urban design of the city. Mijares speaks from his own direct experience of Obregón Santacilia's architecture and its role in the urban order of Mexico City. Antonio Toca Fernández discusses the work of Juan Segura and the portrayal of his work in relationship to the Art Deco movement. Segura's innovative design solutions to complex, modern programs are discussed in terms of their urban design response, formal invention, and careful selection of materials and building systems. The book concludes with Louise Noelle Merles's examination of the architecture and urbanism of Mario Pani. In her essay, she discusses Pani's *multifamiliares* (multifamily) housing projects in terms of their innovation and the unique role of public art within them.

The quality of this body of work in Mexico merits further study. Only the limitations of time and space prevent more detailed explorations. The roles of Hannes Meyer in Mexico, Juan Legarreta, Vladimir Kaspé, Jorge González Reyna, and numerous others are stories that are yet to be told in English. The role of women in the development of Modern architecture in Mexico is a subject for serious study that has virtually been excluded from the existing literature. In particular, the role of women in schools of architecture in Mexico and of women working in the offices of Mario Pani and other notable architects of the time are histories that have yet to be written in English or Spanish.

The Modern architecture of Mexico has not been properly assessed despite the efforts of academic leaders and historians in Mexico, including Antonio Toca Fernández, Louise Noelle Merles, Alberto González Pozo, Ramón Vargas Salguero, Aníbal Figueroa, Pablo Quintero, Humberto Ricalde, Rafael López Rangel, and others, whose anonymous contributions are often unnoticed. Institutions such as the INBA and the Colegio Nacional de Arquitectos de México (CNAM; National College of Mexican Architects) have led the effort to recognize and preserve this vital work. Several schools of architecture in Mexico, including the Universidad Nacional Autónoma de México (UNAM), the Universidad Autónoma Metropolitana (UAM), the Universidad de Guadalajara, the Instituto Tecnológico y de Estudios Superiores de Monterrey (ITESM; Monterrey Institute of Technology and Advanced Studies), as well as the Instituto de Investigaciones Estéticos (IIE; Institute for Aesthetic Research), have actively sponsored research and published work in this area.

The fate of individual early Modern buildings in Mexico is currently a matter of concern for both Mexico and the architectural community at large. I can speak from personal experience of the sad fate of many of the greatest works of this period of architecture in Mexico. For example, in Mexico City, the apartments on the Calle Strasburgo by Enrique de la Mora, Juan O'Gorman's nearby studio for Frances Toor, and the early work of Luis Barragán are tragically the victims of unsympathetic alterations and a lack of a sense of curatorship by their owners. In fact, many of Juan O'Gorman's early projects are now eradicated from the fabric of the city. The question of the preservation of these buildings engages issues of political will, ideology, and resource allocation, among others. It also raises the issue of whether the conservation of the image of modernity ironically reduces the work merely to an aesthetic practice.[4]

Works of architecture are again made present through books, which in turn lead to their reevaluation by academics, practicing architects, governmental authorities, the general public, and their daily users. It is hoped that books such as this will lead to a renewed appreciation of this important body of work, and will ultimately bring about its reassessment as one of the great contributions to the Modern movement.

Edward R. Burian
Los Angeles, August 1994

Notes

1. I have discussed the term "critical," which is used in the Introduction and Postscript, with Steven Moore. Its use here is consistent in many respects with that utilized by Kenneth Frampton as derived from the "Critical Theory" of the Frankfurt School. While the subtleties of this position cannot be completely illuminated here, see the following books for further discussion: D. Held, *Introduction to Critical Theory: Horkheimer to Habermas;* and K. Frampton, "Toward a Critical Theory: Six Points for an Architecture of Resistance," in *The Anti-Aesthetic,* ed. H. Foster, pp. 16–30. However, because this book is a collection of essays by separate authors, each author may use this term with differing intentions.

2. Monographs on individual architects include the following, listed in order of the most recent: P. Heyer, *Abraham Zabludovsky, Architect* (New York: Princeton Architectural Press, 1993); Y. Saito, *Luis Barragán* (Tokyo, Japan: Toto Publishing Co., 1993); A. Salas Portugal, *Barragán* (New York: Rizzoli, 1992); F. González Gortázar, *Conversaciones con Ignacio Díaz Morales sobre Luis Barragán* (Guadalajara: Universidad de Guadalajara, 1992); W. Attoe, *The Architecture of Ricardo Legorreta* (Austin: University of Texas Press, 1990); E. de Anda, *Luis Barragán* (Bogotá: Editorial SomoSur, 1989); R. Auzelle, *Ramírez Vázquez* (Mexico City: Miguel Galas, 1989); R. López Rangel, *Enrique Yáñez en la cultura arquitectónica mexicana* (Mexico City: Editorial Limusa-UAM, 1989); R. Santa María and S. Palleroni, *Carlos Mijares* (Bogotá: Escala, 1989); V. Jiménez, ed., *José Villagrán* (Mexico City: INBA, 1986); M. Larrosa, *Mario Pani* (Mexico City: UNAM, 1985); L. Noelle, *Agustín Hernández, arquitectura y pensamiento* (Mexico City: UNAM/IIE, 1982); P. Vago, *Pedro Ramírez Vázquez, un arquitecto mexicano* (Stuttgart, Germany: Karl Kramer, 1979); E. Ambasz, *The Architecture of Luis Barragán* (New York: Museum of Modern Art, 1976); C. B. Smith, *Builders in the Sun* (New York: Architectural Book Publishing Co., 1967); C. Faber, *Candela: The Shell Builder* (New York: Reinhold Publishing Corp., 1963), among others.

3. Other works in English include H. Beacham's *The Architecture of Mexico: Yesterday and Today* (1969) and a useful brochure edited by S. Kappe and produced at SCIARC, *Modern Architecture, Mexico* (1981). Henry Russell Hitchcock reviews Mexican Modern architecture in *Latin American Architecture Since 1945* (1955) and Issue No. 39 of the Japanese magazine *Process Architecture* (1983).

4. This point was raised by Steven Moore, who thoughtfully commented on the Introduction.

[*Note to the reader.* "Modern" is capitalized when it refers to a specific movement in architectural history (for example, in the terms "Modern architecture," "early Moderns," and "Modern movement"). "Modern" is not capitalized when it is used in the general sense of being characteristic of the present or recent past (as in "modern aesthetics," "modern buildings," or "modern vocabularies"). Following this reasoning, "Functionalism" is capitalized as a specific movement within the broader tradition of Modern Architecture, and the term "functionalist" is not capitalized.]

I

MEXICO, MODERNITY, AND ARCHITECTURE

An Interview with Alberto Pérez-Gómez

[*Note to the reader:* This interview took place at the McGill University School of Architecture in Montreal, Canada, on June 3, 1994, in the offices of the History and Theory of Architecture Program. My goal was to provide an overview and a context for the essays that follow. With this in mind, the scope of our conversation was panoramic, ranging from the origins of modernity in Mexico to the work of specific protagonists in Mexican art and architecture to the impact of the project of modernity on contemporary Mexican culture.

The interview is organized in a roughly chronological order in terms of Mexican history, from the eighteenth century to the present. The conversation begins with an introduction that places modernity in the context of intellectual developments in eighteenth-century Europe and their particular dissemination in Mexico through the Academy of San Carlos. Nineteenth-century Jesuit thought and its effect on secular and architectural culture in Mexico are also reviewed.

The Porfiriato, the École Beaux Arts, and the impact of Positivism and its instrumental relationship to architectural theory are explored. Post-Revolutionary Mexican architectural culture is examined in terms of the role of Juan O'Gorman and Hannes Meyer and the development of the Polytechnic School of Architecture. Modernity's relationship to the aspirations of the Mexican Revolution and its bearing on architectural theory are discussed with particular attention to the writings of José Villagrán García.

Individual architects form the core of the next portion of the interview, with discussions of the work and influence of Mies Van der Rohe and Félix Candela in Mexico. The large public work projects of the 1950s and 1960s are also examined.

Mexican literature and postmodernity are discussed in relationship to modern Mexican architecture. The interview concludes with some comments regarding the utopian notion of the project of modernity, the problem of the obsession with progress, and technological rationalism and its consequences in contemporary Mexican culture.

Many of the ideas and arguments touched upon in the interview are developed in a more complete way in Pérez-Gómez's numerous writings. For a cursory overview regarding many of the points mentioned in the interview, in particular the emergence of modern architectural theory in eighteenth-century Europe, see the introduction to his book *Architecture and the Crisis of Modern Science*. For a broader discussion of the relationship of the body to the conception and experience of architecture, see his article "The Renovation of the Body: John Hejduk and the Cultural Relevance of Theoretical Projects."—Edward R. Burian, Tucson]

Introduction

BURIAN:

In beginning our conversation, we should lay some groundwork regarding the ideological implications of modernity in relationship to Mexico. What is your initial reaction to this topic?

PÉREZ-GÓMEZ:

The question of modernity cannot be simply specified as a chronological condition, like starting at a certain time and ending at a certain time. There is a lot of conversation these days about the end of modernity and where we are going with architecture, particularly in North America and Europe. We have started to realize that "progress" may not be something that has been there forever, but something that we may have invented as a culture, starting in the eighteenth century. So it is interesting to try to think about this and also think about Mexico and where Mexico fits into all of this. Certainly Octavio Paz, particularly in dealing with problems of art and poetry, has very intelligently characterized modernity as a philosophical concept and as a condition that in fact starts in the early nineteenth century after Romanticism, when there is of course a future orientation and a belief in progress and human-generated change. These are the most important characteristics of what one might call modernity. Now, Mexico in the late twentieth century is fundamentally modern in this sense. I think one would have the tendency of misinterpreting many of the fascinating things going on in architecture in Mexico as being "proto-postmodern," anticipating certain features of postmodernism that we witness in North America.

BURIAN:

Are you referring to the popular perception of [Luis] Barragán's work as part of a vernacular tradition? Do you believe that his work is also part of this larger, future-fixated orientation?

PÉREZ-GÓMEZ:

That's right, I think so. I think that ideologically and conceptually, work such as Barragán's fits within the modern world. It's part of the ideology of the Mexican Revolution, it's part of the political agenda that may be changing these days, but as far as we know it's still present. And so I think one has to be precise; philosophically the work is modern. Now, one can then try to differentiate what makes this kind of architecture different from other kinds of Modern architecture . . .

BURIAN:

How does the project of "modernity" occur in Mexico? Is it an idea inherited from Europe?

PÉREZ-GÓMEZ:

In a philosophical sense yes, although most of the time this is not explicit or even spoken about. Modernity is something that Mexico inherits from Europe in the nineteenth century. Concerning questions of architecture and architectural theory, one thing that is particularly clear is that even the more sophisticated attempts to elaborate a theory of architecture in Mexico, such as [José] Villagrán García's, have their immediate origin in the European nineteenth-century mentality, ignoring its long genealogy.

BURIAN:

What are the consequences of the omission of pre-Enlightenment theory in Villagrán's writing?

PÉREZ-GÓMEZ:

The origin of the architectural problematic from Vitruvius to the Renaissance is never present. The consequence of this is that the understanding of theory is fundamentally instrumental. It's a discussion that is meant to have direct consequences for practice, and in that sense, it is modeled on [J. N. L.] Durand and [Julien] Guadet. I don't think there has ever been a critique of this assumption in Mexico. That doesn't mean that there isn't any fascinating architecture in Mexico; on the contrary, there are fantastic buildings! But the origins of this reality come from other sources rather than from a critical understanding of the assumptions taken from the nineteenth century. This is an interesting observation in view of Octavio Paz's remark that the only way one can have an appropriate art and architecture after the nineteenth century is by having a serious critical dimension added to the desire to make poetry or to reveal an order in the world.

BURIAN:

What do you believe are the roots of modernity in Mexico, given the relatively conservative nature of eighteenth- and nineteenth-century Spain?

PÉREZ-GÓMEZ:

The short answer to the question is that the opening to modernity is probably from France, and through an interest in French intellectual development in the nineteenth century. Since the time of the French intervention, Mexico has had an ambivalent relationship with Europe. For example, under the regime of Porfirio Díaz, who was a general of the nationalist Benito Juárez, French urban design and architecture were advocated.

BURIAN:

Can you speak about the Academy of San Carlos and its relationship to French architectural theory? What I find interesting is the Bourbons' ascendancy in Spain and the notion of the Academy of San Carlos becoming a kind of "ministry of taste," in a sense, after its founding in 1785.

PÉREZ-GÓMEZ:

The Academy adopted the system of fine arts as it was interpreted in Spain, and was quite conservative in relation to this system. This is the kind of dissemination of knowledge that would rarely happen through a direct contact. In the twentieth century, there is a knowledge of Guadet—the great writer of the Beaux Arts—in particular, which becomes crucial for the teaching of architecture in the university. For example, my teachers were trained using the Spanish translation of [Giacomo da] Vignola to draw the orders. However, my own school, the Polytechnic, was very much opposed to that pedagogy and instead modeled itself after the Bauhaus.

BURIAN:

For example, in terms of specific buildings, the Hospicio Cabañas by Manuel Tolsá, built at the beginning of the nineteenth century in Guadalajara, has a very gridded plan and a rather austere, stripped and abstracted neoclassical quality. However, it is very seldom discussed as part of the Modern movement in Mexico.

PÉREZ-GÓMEZ:

Yes, and I think that is a problem. Nineteenth-century Neoclassicism is already the result of an understanding that composition could be codified as in modern architectural theory, following

*1.2. Manuel Tolsá,
Hospicio Cabañas
(Cabañas Hospital),
Guadalajara, Jalisco,
established 1801,
facade. Photo by
Edward R. Burian.*

what Durand called a "mechanism of composition." Yes, you are right; one has the sense that what is called Neoclassicism in Mexico, particularly in the nineteenth century, is now a qualified compositional discipline.

Jesuit Thought

in Mexico

BURIAN:

I am particularly struck by the Jesuit education of Miguel Hidalgo and his reading of Rousseau and others. Can you discuss the influence of the Jesuits on intellectual life in eighteenth-century Mexico? In addition, a series of prison projects in Mexico in the nineteenth century recall many of the principles of Durand's treatise and his interest in "prescription and instrumentality." Can you comment on these issues?

PÉREZ-GÓMEZ:

The Jesuits were important everywhere in Latin America and had a great impact on the development of modern architecture in the Western tradition. That's a very big question. Of course we have to place them in the Counter-Reformation, particularly from the mid–sixteenth century onward, and the development related to the Baroque and certain church types that are meant to convince the populace through consensus that the Catholic faith is the correct path. This falls on very fertile ground in Mexico. There is a whole question that I've been studying recently about the Temple of Solomon and [Juan Bautista] Villapando's reconstruction of the temple. He was a Jesuit, a student of [Juan de] Herrera as well as Philip II's architect for the Escorial, and practiced in the second half of the sixteenth century, which roughly corresponds with the beginning of the colonization of Mexico. There is evidence that the Cathedral of Mexico City, for example, is a deliberate evocation of the Temple of Solomon, particularly in its detailing and in the way the towers are placed. The reconstruction of the Temple of Solomon was a particularly Jesuit concern—Philip II was a patron of Villapando's major early-seventeenth-century work on the subject. Of course, the world of European ideals is often realized in the virgin land of Mexico. While the Spaniards founded new cities on gridiron plans and transformed Indian settlements into cities, there is a kind of connection that is always difficult to trace. The Jesuits brought a whole didactic program and political agenda into Mexico, and were also later expelled from Mexico. Of course in the eighteenth century, most people that studied, particularly mestizos and creoles, studied with the Jesuits. After Mexico's independence (and this again comes from the French influence), there was a deliberate separation of church and state. This was from very early on a reaction precisely to the way in which Jesuit politics operated in the eighteenth century. For the Jesuits, the issue of religion was not something that could be separated from the world, but was a part of the way we lived. Perhaps that's why they were so interested in education and why they have always had a social agenda. At the same time, this made them very problematic for the government, so from the beginning of the Mexican Republic this very "modern" separation was instituted. In relation to your previous question and your observations of the prisons, I think what is interesting are not only the compositional methods in nineteenth-century Mexico, which are obviously similar to those that are coming out of the École de Beaux Arts, but also the institutions, such as prisons and hospitals, which are really modern French inventions. These institutions are adopted by the Mexican government in the nineteenth century. So at that level you can see very clearly how architecture partakes of the same concern, even though the connection may not be through primary sources, like the direct knowledge of Durand, for example.

BURIAN:
Do you think the Jesuits laid the groundwork for modernity or actually introduced modern theory to Mexico?

PÉREZ-GÓMEZ:
You see, that's the thing about the Jesuits: their relationship to modernity is a very ambivalent condition and very hard to dis-

1.3. Diego Rivera, detail of The Legacy of Independence *mural at the National Palace, Mexico City, 1929–1930. Photo by Elena E. Abrahamsson B.*

cuss in a few words. For example, to go back to Villapando: He would insist that the architect is someone who has nothing to do with practical matters, his is purely an intellectual discipline. He's very radical about this because he is identifying with the Augustinian architect. He goes much further in this direction than anybody else in the late sixteenth century, in saying architecture is *about theory!* If you think about that, and about how we understand architecture after the École Polytechnique, after the French Revolution, and you assume that an architect is someone that goes to a university to study a theoretical discipline, you can see a connection. Of course, that's not the way that Villapando meant it. For him, it was a theological issue, and yet he was one of the first to actually state that the discipline of architecture is purely theoretical. There is that dimension in Jesuit thought that is very modern because once this model of the architect as scientist (as a knower of truth) becomes secularized, you are right into modernity, i.e., the architect as the guide who controls and plans.

BURIAN:
This is very interesting . . . you almost describe it as a kind of priesthood that becomes secularized.

PÉREZ-GÓMEZ:
That's right.

BURIAN:
Can you talk a little about that?

PÉREZ-GÓMEZ:
Well, I think that's the issue here. That's why the Jesuits have such an amazing history. They can convert or be converted. You know, for example, that in the seventeenth century the Jesuit missions in China were recalled because the Chinese were converting them. This is almost on the verge of being completely modern. You are evangelizing, you are trying to convert, but at the same time you are so connected to the culture and the specific political orders of certain places that you get converted yourself. That is why the issue is so fascinating. In *official* Mexican history, the account is black and white: The Jesuits were religious people who were intervening in the government, and they had to be excluded. But as you know, Miguel Hidalgo was educated by Jesuits, and this is truly symptomatic of the ambiguities that constitute Mexico's political and cultural history in the nineteenth century.

Positivism, the

École de Beaux

Arts, and the

Idea of

Instrumentality

BURIAN:
Patrick Romanell, in *The Making of the Mexican Mind,* discusses the influence of [Auguste] Comte on Mexican Positivism, stating: "Barreda had tremendous faith in a scientific education because he saw in its intellectual order the very 'key' to the social and moral order which Mexico so badly needed . . . but . . . the only scientific tradition taken seriously . . . was mathematics . . . a neutral science which could reorganize society." Could you comment on the Positivism of the Porfirio Díaz administration and

the subsequent rational, progressive art and architecture they tried to establish as part of the secularization of Mexican life?

PÉREZ-GÓMEZ:
Political Positivism, yes, I think that is perhaps an interesting way of putting it. Porfirio Díaz has often been maligned by official historians in Mexico. Positivism is probably a good way to describe his ideological framework, in which the issue was finally the clear establishment of Mexican political life as secular, and a complete separation from the church. This was something that he made very explicit and part of his entire program, adopting a progressive notion of history. So at this point we are sure that Mexico is completely thrown into modernity.

BURIAN:
And the notion was that the embracing of the Beaux Arts was the way to do this in architecture?

PÉREZ-GÓMEZ:
Absolutely! This explains your quotation of Barreda almost a hundred years after similar pedagogical programs were introduced in the schools in Paris, and about fifty years after Comte. It is obvious that someone like Barreda could speak in these terms, that scientific education is what it is all about. Comte had stated that the new aristocrat was the engineer, and his discipline was descriptive geometry. Mexico embraced this notion by the late nineteenth century. At the end of the century it's very clear that the whole agenda of the French Beaux Arts, including its instrumentality, is what drives Mexican architects.

BURIAN:
Could you talk about instrumentality and what you mean by its consequence?

PÉREZ-GÓMEZ:
The issue is that theory, rather than being primarily about sources of ethical action, becomes applied science. Basically, that's what I mean by instrumentality. In traditional architectural theories—which is precisely what Mexican theoreticians even in the twentieth century have never really looked at very carefully— it is very clear that the issue is a discourse that has the status of philosophy, it's an explanation of how certain things make sense in the realm of practice. It's not about *how* to do things nor

1.4. Enrique de la Mora, apartment building on Calle Strasburgo, Mexico City, 1934. Photo courtesy of the Archive of Louise Noelle Merles.

about a *method* to do things, is not about the direct applicability of the discourse. Instrumentality signals the desire for a direct applicability of the discourse. That is why Barreda can be so fascinated with mathematics as the science that would allow you to rationalize everything, from construction to social issues.

BURIAN:
Are you primarily talking about a kind of methodology, as opposed to merely proportional methods?

PÉREZ-GÓMEZ:
That's right.

Vasconcelos

and Caso

BURIAN:
Let's turn our attention to post-Revolutionary culture and to the Mexican philosophers José Vasconcelos, "an appreciator of fine arts," and Antonio Caso, "an appreciator of morals." Vasconcelos claimed that a "new Ulysses" was the model for post-Revolutionary Mexican society, in contrast to what he called "the Anglo-Saxon pragmatic," or trained worker in craft. Vasconcelos also proposed an educational system based on learning for its own sake and was at the forefront of the Mexican Mural movement. Could you comment on these two protagonists of post-Revolutionary Mexican culture?

PÉREZ-GÓMEZ:
Caso and Vasconcelos are far richer than they have been made to be by their commentators and disciples. In general, one could say that both are reacting against a kind of Positivism, because they feel that this understanding of knowledge is reductive. Caso is of course interested in morality and ethics. Vasconcelos believed in the idea that aesthetic education would actually bring together the differing views of the people, would unify the political intentions in Mexico, and would actually result in a more coherent way of life. He saw art as a powerful political device. Because of this I think you are right, he had a profound impact on all the politically driven art of the post-Revolutionary era, particularly the Mural movement.

BURIAN:
I think that there is a tendency to link the post-Revolutionary functionalist architects with the muralists, who I believe are actually quite different in many respects.

PÉREZ-GÓMEZ:

They are quite different, yet often believed to be driven by the same ideology. This is also a complicated problem. That is why Vasconcelos's writings were so passionately debated, either hated or loved by the generation that precedes mine, particularly in the circles of people interested in building and constructing things, such as engineers, architects, and artists.

1.5. Enrique del Moral, Mario Pani, and Salvador Ortega Flores; wall detail of Rector's Tower, Ciudad Universitaria (University City), Mexico City, 1950–1952. Photo by Edward R. Burian.

The Polytechnic,

Hannes Meyer,

and

Juan O'Gorman

BURIAN:

It is interesting to think about the Polytechnic in relationship to Vasconcelos's vision of education in Mexico. What was the role of the humanities in this curriculum?

PÉREZ-GÓMEZ:

I would first like to clarify the kind of education that the Polytechnic proposed. It was, of course, a very technical education that was conceived as an alternative to the more artistic education of the university. Curiously, at the Polytechnic we had as many design courses as anyone at the university, but the issue was that somehow, in a very vague way, there was a formal ability cultivated in the university that was rather suspect in the Polytechnic. I suppose the Polytechnic had greater emphasis on technical subjects, such as structural design and things like that, and even a greater aversion for the humanities. However, I think that in a certain way, particularly in the sixties when I was going to school, the programs were similar despite their programmatic or stated differences.

BURIAN:

Could you elaborate on Hannes Meyer and his role at the Polytechnic and as a planner in Mexico?

PÉREZ-GÓMEZ:

Hannes Meyer envisioned that the architect had to be responsible for a technological architecture of science, one that might propose an alternative for a way of life in the future that would further or imply a transformed human consciousness. Of course, his view was connected to transformations expected from a Marxist project of history, with its de-centering of the self, and its project for a socialist community. He brought that with him to the Polytechnic, and he marked the school profoundly. Proposals that could be approved as thesis projects needed to have a "social relevance," rather than a theoretical or an aesthetic relevance. This became a particular concern of the Polytechnic School of Architecture.

BURIAN:

Was Juan O'Gorman also involved in establishing the Polytechnic School of Architecture?

PÉREZ-GÓMEZ:

Certainly, O'Gorman and Hannes Meyer were. They were convinced that it would be possible to make an architecture out of a social consciousness and related to a political agenda.

BURIAN:
Can you clarify the relationship between social consciousness and technical rationalism?

PÉREZ-GÓMEZ:
That's really part of Hannes Meyer's inheritance, the idea that a *truly* functional architecture, a rational architecture, would be better suited to fulfill the minimum basic requirements of the Mexican population, furthering social equality. This is more than socialism. Originally it was inspired by rather radical communist views, so that somehow by implementing technological rationalism you could create conditions for a new man to develop. This is very clear in Hannes Meyer's work, and deemed appropriate by the ideological inheritors of the Mexican Revolution.

BURIAN:
If you examine O'Gorman's writings in the 1930s, it seems that his understanding of Le Corbusier implies a *very* selective reading.

PÉREZ-GÓMEZ:
You are absolutely right! That's a very important thing to observe. O'Gorman *is* reading Le Corbusier selectively; his interest in Ville Radieuse and in technology all fit well within his conception of the Polytechnic. So in this case you have a kind of architecture that is technological, but that is meant to continue the political project of the Revolution. These things come together neatly. Vasconcelos might have opposed this, yet for him, *art* also had a political agenda. Thus, the differences between mural painting and architecture (despite their concerns for examining the same questions) were also quite pronounced.

BURIAN:
It's interesting to think about Le Corbusier's murals in his architecture in relation to the Mexican notion of *integración plástica*. I believe there are two ways to view this: one, which I previously mentioned, was the "Mexicanization" of Le Corbusier's murals, which were an integral part of his architecture; the other was the strategy of making functionalist architecture palpable to Mexicans by imbuing this work with more iconographic and didactic content.

PÉREZ-GÓMEZ:

The crucial question for mural painting, besides the connection with the past, is the political agenda, the belief that somehow you can actually change society by making painting that is about communist ideals. There is a real belief in this agenda in the work of [David Alfaro] Siqueiros and [Diego] Rivera for example.

BURIAN:

It is interesting also that it became an official government art. Do you think that Functionalism also became an official government architecture for public projects, for modern projects like hospitals and airports?

1.6. Pedro Ramírez Vázquez and Rafael Mijares; Secretaría de Relaciones Exteriores (Ministry of Foreign Relations), Plaza of the Three Cultures, Tlatelolco, Mexico City, 1964–1965. Photo by Edward R. Burian.

PÉREZ-GÓMEZ:

Well, yes, in a certain way. When I think of the great urban projects like Tlatelolco, I think that is probably so. It's the idea that somehow you strip everything to the minimum in order to be able to give more to all. The agenda of the Revolution was to split up the country and give a piece of land to every single per-

son. Yet the architecture that came out of the university was increasingly associated with the powerful classes, with people who had the means to build in a more elaborate way.

BURIAN:
In thinking about mural painting, the famous 1939 Siqueiros mural for the Syndicate for Electrical Workers, entitled *Retrato de la Burguesía* [Picture of the bourgeoisie], is particularly fascinating. It has both the rational system of gridding for the windows and the wall enclosure system, and also tremendous spatial, twisted, primal forces emerging from the painting.

PÉREZ-GÓMEZ:
It's all about the Mexican way of life. It's all about Mexican craft, about all the rituals that are always there, about celebration of death, about the many things that are embedded in the *mestizaje* of Indian and Spanish blood. Perhaps this allows the functional building to work together with a mural to establish some kind of political and rhetorical space. I think O'Gorman particularly understood how these things could be brought together.

BURIAN:
The mural painted by Siqueiros in 1952 for the Zone 1 Hospital of the Mexican Social Security Institute tends to break down surfaces of what's flat and what's not. There are several ways of understanding this work. One is that the mural is merely an appliqué; another, which one sees over and over in commentaries on the history of Mexican art, is the notion of the continuity of a pre-Columbian or Baroque tradition. Another way of understanding this work is in the background of a term used insistently by Ruth Rivera: *integración plástica*. It seems this term is used not merely as a formal device but as an innately Mexican quality.

PÉREZ-GÓMEZ:
As you said, that is also my feeling. This is an operative notion that has worked well to bring together the pre-Columbian reality of Mexico in terms of its ethnicity, and the program of Modern architecture. This particular case [the mural at the Zone 1 Hospital] is an example where a desire to integrate an irretrievable past translates into an ethical concern for the presence of Indian blood vis-à-vis the reality of the stringency of modern functional programs.

Modernity and the Idea of Revolution

BURIAN:
Octavio Paz makes the following point in his book *Essays on Mexican Art:* "One of the distinctive traits of the Mexican Revolution was the absence—relatively speaking—of an ideology that was also a universal vision of the world and society. Comparison with the English Revolution of the seventeenth century, with the American and French revolutions at the end of the eighteenth or with Russia in the twentieth will spare me a long demonstration. . . . *We did not have a metahistory* [italics in original] . . . the Marxism of Rivera and his comrades had no other meaning than that of replacing the absence of philosophy in the Mexican Revolution with an international revolutionary history." Do you substantially agree with this view?

PÉREZ-GÓMEZ:
Yes, that's obvious, it's true. [José] Ortega y Gasset, the most important twentieth-century Spanish philosopher, wrote that the only *real* revolution was the French Revolution; other upheavals have been mostly revolts.

BURIAN:
Paz calls the Mexican Revolution a revolt as well.

PÉREZ-GÓMEZ:
Yes, I would tend to agree with that. That's obvious. Now whether that projects directly on mural painting, I think that is another issue, perhaps more complicated. . . . I believe Vasconcelos only partially understood that Marxism was merely replacing an absence of an overriding philosophy of the Mexican Revolution with an international revolutionary history . . . I guess for artists this is fair. There is always this problem of the theory and practice of Mexican art and architecture. That is a fundamental question. There is a certain dimension of Mexican artistic production that comes from the gut: the power to make, which is totally connected to the earth, to the food, to the culture, and which cannot be reduced to ideological or theoretical considerations. That's perhaps what "saves" the ideological art of the Revolution, as well as, if I may put it this way, Mexican art and architecture. I suppose in the end it's precisely the making and its sensuous qualities that have priority over conceptual issues.

BURIAN:
Do you mean at the level of craft and materials?

PÉREZ-GÓMEZ:
At the level of craft, yes, all of that, all of those things that are involved in putting together a work. So while the ideology of Rivera and Siqueiros is rather shallow in their naive Marxism, the reality of the work is something else. I would question the very premise that the work of art can be determined by a political program. The work is potent because it speaks beyond this kind of ideological shallowness that Paz discloses.

BURIAN:
Do you think the ideological development of mural painting is different than the impulses that led to the functionalist movement in architecture in Mexico in the 1930s? Is it reasonable to discuss painting and architecture in Mexico in the thirties and forties as responses to a similar ideological, conceptual, or aesthetic agenda?

PÉREZ-GÓMEZ:
I think that they are connected by this political agenda.

BURIAN:
But certainly not in terms of formal devices, such as Cubist devices?

PÉREZ-GÓMEZ:
No, in that sense, no, not at all.

Modern

Architecture in

Mexico and

Symbolic Order

BURIAN:
You have spoken about "a meaningful symbolic order" in your writings. Do you think that the fusion of murals and modern architecture begins to create that kind of presence?

PÉREZ-GÓMEZ:
Possibly . . . However, what I still miss in most Mexican architecture is an understanding of the program, of the temporal dimension of the building, that might synthesize this tradition. That's always been much more difficult, because it has to do with the reality of two cultures—the pre-Columbian culture and the Spanish culture—intimately intertwined yet distinct. Juárez was an Indian, and president of Mexico in the nineteenth century, yet today class and race distinctions still matter. It's a mind-boggling thing. The recent development with the Zapatista move-

ment and the lack of justice that many native people actually endure is a reality we cannot deny. The problem is serious in terms of the bringing together of certain cultural strands that are *not* truly integrated when it comes to fundamental values. The two cultures have really not come together completely. Current traditions are often antithetical to the programs of the government regarding efficiency and progress. A good example is the idea of universal education, with no regard for the hundreds of Indian languages or cultural realities that are part of the country. The situation is truly ambivalent. On one hand, the government is very modern, with no involvement of the church, and there is progress and social justice. But on the other hand, there is an elite of technocrats that control the situation and that in fact would do all that is in their power to avoid a truly respectful integration. Given all these paradoxes, when one talks about symbolic order, perhaps the closest possible approximation is indeed the formal "plastic integration" mentioned by Ruth Rivera.

BURIAN:
What is interesting about the Mexican Mural movement is its engagement with difficult, tense, very primal *issues!*

PÉREZ-GÓMEZ:
This painting does seem to speak about the pre-Columbian Mexican tradition. It is useful to recall that the Jesuits and Franciscans brought certain programs to New Spain and that Indian craftsmanship produced beautiful *retablos,* far superior to many in Spain. In some ways, the work is naive; however, it has a power and earthiness that is undeniable.

Modern Architecture in Mexico and Its Relationship to Theory

BURIAN:
Let's talk a little about the formal devices. What I find extraordinary is that for all of the admiration for Le Corbusier's work in Mexico, there is very little Cubist development in architecture in Mexico. You don't understand the free plan or free section. You don't understand the kind of collapsing of things in a Cubist way as described by Colin Rowe and others. Is it that this generation of Mexican architects were not interested in theory, or that they didn't understand these issues?

PÉREZ-GÓMEZ:
No, not at all, you are absolutely right.

BURIAN:
So is it not being interested in the theory?

PÉREZ-GÓMEZ:
I think that is what it is. I think that Le Corbusier is misread mostly, as we mentioned before, for his "optimism" about how architecture can engage technology through a sort of functional determinism to make a brave new world. I don't think I have ever come across a theoretical discussion of the full scope of Le Corbusier's work in the context of Mexican architectural education. All the implications of Le Corbusier as an artist, the whole philosophical framework that drives Le Corbusier, all that is completely disregarded. I would speculate that things like *Le Poéme de L'Angle Droit* and all the more poetic aspects of Le Corbusier were probably not known in Mexico, certainly not known by all those people that thought they were being influenced by him. What early Modern Mexican architects took from Le Corbusier, and generally from Functionalism, was a set of *reduced* compositional devices that were already there in the Beaux Arts. You strip ornament away, you keep the same devices, but you are still working in plan with a gridded sheet of paper. You may remember how Le Corbusier insists that students of architecture have to start with a gridded sheet of paper. That's the Le Corbusier that Mexicans import. Design becomes the resolution of the plan in terms of a functional diagram with some flare and a wonderful craft. The whole "other" dimension of Le Corbusier as an artist is not really understood, particularly the struggle to integrate the "plastic search" into the work of architecture. The difficulty is to understand that this is *not* one thing that is attached to the other, that you don't have a painter that attaches his work to a functional building, but rather that this struggle actually changes the possibilities of ideation and conception of architecture itself—that is what I generally find missing. It's interesting that Mexican architects, until recently, have hardly ever used axonometrics as a design tool. There are certain representational devices that we never touched in school. We usually worked in plan, section, elevation, and perspective. So it's really a kind of Beaux Arts stripped of ornament. This is what I find fascinating and paradoxical.

BURIAN:
You seldom see the crossover between mural painting and architecture in terms of spatial devices.

PÉREZ-GÓMEZ:
Very seldom, it's always like two autonomous things that are supposed to be integrated, like Rivera says, but in fact remain autonomous.

BURIAN:
Could you discuss the differences between "functionalist theory" in Europe and the United States and in Mexico?

PÉREZ-GÓMEZ:
Functionalist theory in Mexico is reduced to bubble diagrams and to use. And I'm not sure that even today in the United States there is a clear understanding of where Functionalism as a metaphor, as a scientific metaphor, comes from. The mathematical origin of the idea of function and the older use of function as representation, or *función pública,* are not even part of the agenda. What twentieth-century architects mean by Functionalism, and what Mexican architects understand as functional architecture, is simply the idea that somehow all that matters is the resolution of the programmatic questions as economically and efficiently as possible so that form might "follow," excluding the architect's potential to indulge his imagination. That is what is meant by Functionalism, certainly, if you read Villagrán García or others. In summary, the great difference for architectural theory in Mexico is disconnection from its sources. Durand's text in Europe emerged from the tradition of architectural treatises, even if it questioned its genealogy. The problem in Mexico, and probably also in the United States, was a total lack of understanding of the roots of these problems, as if things had always been like that, so that there is no reason to look to these other aspects of the tradition, such as going back to Vitruvius, to figure out where all that is coming from and to try to understand where we stand and what it all means. It's as if what is being handed down to us is completely self-evident. I think that's the fundamental distinction, and the reality of most colonial places, and in a way this is a colonial knowledge, particularly when it comes to the theories.

BURIAN:
I believe that the terms "Modernism" and "Functionalism" are used interchangeably when discussing work in early twentieth-century Mexico, when in fact they are really quite distinct. One *aspect* of Modernism is Functionalism, as well as Cubism, Surrealism, and other movements.

1.7. Mario Pani, Ciudad Habitacional Nonoalco-Tlatelolco (Nonoalco-Tlatelolco Urban Housing Project), Mexico City, 1964. Photo courtesy of the Archive of Louise Noelle Merles.

PÉREZ-GÓMEZ:
Exactly, absolutely.

BURIAN:
And I think that these other movements didn't gain a kind of "theoretical toehold" in Mexico, at least in terms of architecture.

PÉREZ-GÓMEZ:
Absolutely. Looking at the works of art, however, one gains other insights. As you know, André Breton was very fascinated with Mexico and its cultural traditions. So there were influences the other way around. But within the discourse of architectural theory the "critical" dimension of modernity has never really had an impact, at least not until after my years as a student there in the early seventies.

BURIAN:
Could you comment about the program of vocational schools—

35

which I believe are very impressive in terms of their social agenda—designed by O'Gorman after the Revolution? Were O'Gorman's numerous manifestos written in the 1930s being studied in schools of architecture in Mexico, particularly the Polytechnic?

PÉREZ-GÓMEZ:
In regard to the manifestos of O'Gorman, perhaps they were read earlier, but not in my time. Certainly the vocational schools designed by O'Gorman are some of the most extraordinarily austere schools *ever* designed. They are absolutely stripped down.

BURIAN:
Absolutely . . . in O'Gorman's words, "the maximum result for the minimum effort."

PÉREZ-GÓMEZ:
The vocational schools demonstrate the connection between Functionalism and the social program of education for the people. It was supposed to be a whole autonomous system of preparatory schools for the Polytechnic with an emphasis on techniques such as foundry, carpentry, welding, etc. This is the kind of very sophisticated technical education with *total* exclusion of the humanities, which of course is very problematic.

BURIAN:
O'Gorman later in his life commented that it was unfortunate that it was Le Corbusier and not [Frank Lloyd] Wright who impressed early Moderns in Mexico, as Wright's work was uniquely connected to the land and its place . . . he called Taliesin West the great work of Modern architecture in North America. Could you comment on this?

PÉREZ-GÓMEZ:
O'Gorman's vision of Le Corbusier is a complex one. When he realized that Le Corbusier was becoming a kind of reductive recipe for certain practitioners, producing rather nasty, minimal architecture that was really inhuman, he decided to give it up. I believe the invocation of Wright has more to do with his own changing sensibilities as an artist than with a deep understanding of what Wright was about.

BURIAN:
Did engineers or even architects gain a kind of political ascendancy? Were they running for public office?

PÉREZ-GÓMEZ:
Yes, they did. This was the beginning of the technocracy that has definitely dominated Mexican politics recently. [Note to the reader: In 1995, the new president of Mexico, Ernesto Zedillo, is a graduate of the Polytechnic in Mexico. He also holds a Ph.D. in economics from Yale.]

BURIAN:
Did they believe they could solve all social problems by rational means?

PÉREZ-GÓMEZ:
Oh absolutely! It was supposed to be for everyone and for the betterment of Mexico. In fact, my father's generation very much held that belief. The best profession was engineering; other disciplines were considered inferior. Technology is still rampant, so I guess from that point of view, there is still something to say about Vasconcelos! (But one has to take that with "a grain of salt.")

Villagrán García and the Dissemination of Modernist Theory in Mexico

BURIAN:
What role did José Villagrán García play in the formulation of modern architectural theory in Mexico? Could you comment on the content and order of Villagrán García's book *Teoría de la arquitectura?*

PÉREZ-GÓMEZ:
If we look at architectural theory in a historical context, there have been editions of Vitruvius in libraries in Mexico City since the sixteenth century. However, the theoretical understanding of practitioners during the colonial period was not very sophisticated. In a sense, a tradition was imported from Spain and adapted to local craftsmanship. In the twentieth century, Villagrán García was the most important modern theoretician at the Universidad Nacional. Villagrán's theory itself is rather eclectic, yet also quite original in certain ways in terms of the way things are put together.

BURIAN:
Could you expand on that, please?

PÉREZ-GÓMEZ:
Even though his *Teoría de la arquitectura* is not very clear in the way the chapters are set out, the conceptualization of the theory is taken almost directly as a structure from Vitruvius. There is a

tendency to propose eclectic, critical readings of certain assumptions that come from Vitruvius; for example, you find a whole chapter on optical correction and a whole chapter on proportion, which are issues that Vitruvius spoke about and have a certain pedigree in the tradition of architectural theory. What is lacking is an understanding of the issues he discusses in relation to changing worldviews. For example, there is an issue regarding how optical correction becomes very important at the end of the seventeenth century in the work of [Charles] Perrault. Perrault criticizes optical correction because he believes it's a way for architects to justify the discrepancy that exists between the proportions that appear in a text in theory, and the ones that are made in the building in practice. So he believes it is already an excuse and that somehow we should get rid of this idea of optical correction in architectural theory. Perrault wants to get closer to a more *instrumental* theory of architecture, whereas Vitruvius, in fact, had another meaning altogether. For Vitruvius the issue was that the perception of the building had to be as *perfect* as possible. So what optical correction took into account was the deception that was caused by the eye. So it was a kind of "anti-perspective," where the issue is that the eye is *not* perfect, it conveys distorted information and for that reason you have to make some adjustments in the way the building is actually proportioned for the work to convey its perfect regularity through embodied experience, which is how one engages with the building in everyday life. These kinds of subtleties are critical, and are not understood *at all* by Villagrán.

BURIAN:
So Villagrán is really going back to his Beaux Arts training in the formation of his theory?

PÉREZ-GÓMEZ:
Yes, there is a lot of that there.

BURIAN:
I agree. What is also astonishing are the topics of the chapters, which include *three* chapters devoted to proportions!

PÉREZ-GÓMEZ:
Yes, and they are very strange chapters, because he is trying to discuss proportions in relation to utility, but he also acknowledges that there is a kind of aesthetic dimension to proportions

that he never really fully states. There is a kind of remnant of Renaissance theory; however, during the Renaissance proportions made sense in terms of a cosmological understanding that obviously has nothing to do with twentieth-century Mexico. His thesis is indeed eclectic. There are countless concepts of Functionalism taken from reading Le Corbusier, together with aspects of the Beaux Arts that are simply brought together. Toward the end of his life he became interested in [Martin] Heidegger's "dwelling," but I could never grasp how all this was meant to become a coherent position.

BURIAN:
Could you comment on his chapter on "character?"

PÉREZ-GÓMEZ:
The interest of architects regarding character has its origins in eighteenth-century French theory. It happens at a time when there are some questions concerning the traditional understanding of architectural meaning, when it's no longer very clear that, for example, proportions or geometrical manipulations can actually ensure that the building is a "small world," a microcosm of the universe. When these questions emerge in the history of Western architecture, then there appears a complementary or alternative discourse that is generally connected to language. In the French tradition, people start discussing why buildings don't have enough "character." They are no longer meaningful enough. Of course the question of character has different modalities, some connected to traditional literary modes (Germain Boffrand), others to the character of nature (Etienne-Louis Boullée). Eventually character becomes associated with the appropriateness to the use of the building. In [Claude-Nicolas] Ledoux there is still a metaphoric relationship between the form and the use. It's not as if one determines the other. But there is an awareness that somehow the building has to be endowed with a character consistent with the use that it is given. In the nineteenth century, character becomes associated with function. In a way, what Durand says is the opposite of Ledoux. Ledoux believed architects should be very concerned with character; Durand, in contrast, thought that the architect should not be concerned with character at all—as long as the planning was right, the character would simply follow. Villagrán thinks the whole issue of character relates essentially to questions of use. He completely disregards the roots of the problem prior to the nineteenth century. Hence, he

sees character as one aspect of architectural meaning separate from other psychological or aesthetic components. He would argue that a building can be beautiful, but may not have the appropriate character. He's talking about use. In fact, it has nothing to do with Mexican character as a "regional" expression. He says, for example, that a temple front can be used in Europe or North America for a bank; a Greek temple and the American building could both have nice proportions, they could both be beautiful, yet in one case the character is appropriate, while in the other one it's not. This is a very Kantian way of looking at categories, isolating them and then separating out certain aspects of meaning in order to analyze them, implying that they have a kind of autonomous reality. I would claim that's a very problematic way of looking at the questions of architectural meaning. One has to realize that the meaning of architecture is something that you cannot simply pull apart or control as if it were composed of additive factors. You have aesthetic proportions, you have other kinds of proportions, you have character here, you have use there, you bring it all together, you shake it, and you have architecture. Do you see the problem?

Modernity and the Pre-Columbian Past

BURIAN:
Could you comment on attempts on the part of modern architects in Mexico to integrate pre-Columbian ornament, massing, or scales of public space in their work?

PÉREZ-GÓMEZ:
It's very hard to generalize. I think that it's always a question of appropriateness to a specific building task, to a specific intention. I think that, clearly, if I have a problem, it's purely a formal conceit. Really, it depends on the context . . .

BURIAN:
I think that particularly in projects like the Ciudad Universitaria, the terracing and the scale of the plazas attempt to make reference to pre-Columbian strategies. What is your sense of this work?

PÉREZ-GÓMEZ:
It is in some respects a successful example of how certain sensibilities can be translated into a contemporary program. I don't feel that I'm walking on the pyramids, and at the same time, I

can recognize that it's Mexican. So when it works that way, I have absolutely no problem with it.

BURIAN:
In many of your writings, you talk about a building's users having a "deep sense of recognition." Do you think that happens at the Ciudad Universitaria?

PÉREZ-GÓMEZ:
Maybe. But I have a sense that younger generations, certainly in the 1960s, tended to perceive some of that work as truly oppressive and at odds with their own socialist ideals.

BURIAN:
For me, in this case, it doesn't become merely an appliqué. I think the mural programs that we discussed earlier and the terracing are very successful. In his book, Pedro Ramírez Vázquez describes his screens around the edge of the courtyard at the Museo Nacional de Antropología e Historia [National Museum of Anthropology and History] in terms of making a reference to Mayan architecture. At the Ciudad Universitaria, the terracing and the materiality of the volcanic stone is one of the most successful aspects of the urban design.

PÉREZ-GÓMEZ:
Yes. That's of course a part of the craft. The craftsman's *savoir faire* is very real and still present in Mexico, although this may be changing. This is one of the aspects that makes contemporary architecture in Mexico such a fascinating thing. The craftsman takes pride in his work, the work is not just labor, there is a love for the craft; and that of course is what postindustrial countries have a very hard time finding. That gives, in my view, a quality to the building environment in general that has *nothing* to do with how many bright ideas anybody had, or how theoretical or sophisticated the *maestro de obras* may be . . . you know what I mean? At that level, Mexico is *rich*. The *basic* reason for the fascination we have for Mexican architecture is precisely craft, rather than any kind of sophisticated understanding of the tradition of theory. That's my feeling, and of course there are some exceptions. You mentioned the Ciudad Universitaria, you mentioned Ramírez Vázquez and the Museo Nacional de Antropología e Historia. I think that clearly there are some really interesting works where there is a much more subtle and successful

1.8. Pedro Ramírez Vázquez, Jorge Campuzano, and Rafael Mijares; National Museum of Anthropology and History, Mexico City, 1963. Photo by Edward R. Burian.

attempt at translating certain experience of the past, precisely because it's a constructed experience as well. The Museo Nacional de Antropología e Historia is extremely successful as a program. I find it a delightful museum to visit . . . it has a rhythm . . . it's just great. These, among others, are certainly some works that would live up to what Kenneth Frampton has called successful "critical regionalism."

BURIAN:
I think what is interesting about that discussion is the difference between a regional architecture that responds to place, climate, and contemporary tectonics as opposed to a regional architecture that is merely "visual" and imitates the forms of nostalgic tectonics, but is unconnected to the climate or contemporary tectonics or labor practices. Virtually *every* book on Modern architecture of the period includes a summary of pre-Columbian architecture. Could you comment on this as both an intellectual construct and a cultural phenomenon and also within the tradition of "modern" architectural literature, which lays claim to and justifies its work in relation to an older, more mythic civilization—in other words, even within technological rationality, a mythic sensibility is required?

PÉREZ-GÓMEZ:
This is a very interesting question. You are absolutely right that

there is always a chapter on pre-Columbian architecture. We had
a whole one-year course on the history of pre-Columbian architecture at the Polytechnic.

BURIAN:
Was pre-Columbian architecture discussed in terms of an analogy regarding processes or tools?

PÉREZ-GÓMEZ:
Not usually. There is always a kind of explicit or implicit connection that is made between the pre-Columbian heritage and modern Mexico. I think there are different dimensions to this. At a
certain level, it's a sort of mythical history of the country, whose
origins have to be actualized after a messy period of colonial architecture and foreign influences in the nineteenth century, and
now we are "back on track." That sounds kind of nice, but we
know very well when we look at the social reality of Mexico that
Indians still have a very tough time. Thus the use of this mythical
construct to validate or legitimate Mexican cultural autonomy is
full of contradictions.

BURIAN:
In the nineteenth century, José Obregón painted classicized versions of a pre-Columbian past, depicted for example in his painting *The Discovery of Pulque,* of 1869. Can you discuss the issue
of legitimizing one's architectural culture by appealing to an
older tradition?

PÉREZ-GÓMEZ:
That's a very old model. I think what is particular about Mexico
is the tendency to exclude European history, emphasizing a connection with pagan origins that nobody believes in anymore. In
a curious way it's a dead tradition, yet the Christian tradition is
not dead completely, so it's always a "hot potato." As you know,
public religious manifestations are forbidden by law, yet we have
some of the largest processions in the world in honor of Our
Lady of Guadalupe. What might then be the meaning of this particular Mexican understanding of Modern architecture to reconnect it to its pre-Columbian roots? It's certainly not about
technique . . .

BURIAN:
In some cases it's formal.

PÉREZ-GÓMEZ:
Yes, in some cases it's formal.

BURIAN:
It's an issue of character, and in some cases it's an issue of national identity. What about the problem of a national architecture? When does this appear as a problem in architectural theory?

PÉREZ-GÓMEZ:
Well, as a problem, as a subconscious problem, I believe it's a nineteenth-century problem. I don't think it appears anywhere before that time. I think it probably emerges in relation to nationalism in music, in literature, and with the idea of autonomous nations. Mexico is a modern nation since 1810. Hence, the concern for what is authentic Mexican architecture is not surprising. On the other hand, Mexico has always exhibited a great confidence in the strength of its culture. Paranoia does not exist regarding foreign influence. Mexicans believe that what happens in Mexico is Mexican. It's totally appropriated.

BURIAN:
Colonial work as well?

PÉREZ-GÓMEZ:
Colonial work as well. And I think the reason for this is the old *mestizaje,* the fact that Mexican and European cultures started to come together from the beginning. So while there is this complex social reality in late twentieth-century Mexico, there is also, I think, less of a "hang-up" about what is Mexican and what isn't. There is a base for action, there is a kind of tradition of making that goes deeper than in other North American cultures. So there is a greater self-confidence. Things may have changed in the last few years, but I would be very surprised to find discussion about this being a problem in Mexico. The perception that somehow modernity and tradition flow into each other and become Mexican is probably the norm.

BURIAN:
Do you think in this sense Modern architecture becomes "Mexican?"

PÉREZ-GÓMEZ:
Yes, it's really an appropriation made by selective memory and cultural amnesia.

Mies van der

Rohe and Mexico

BURIAN:

I believe that many of Barragán's compositions, particularly the plan manipulations, are absolutely Miesian, although the materials and tectonics are vernacular and belong to the place. I also think his buildings are conceived as a perspectival, cinegraphic sequence, not merely as syntactic exercises in plan. Could you tell me why the Miesian sensibility never seemed to gain ascendancy in Mexico? Was it simply because of the tectonic limitations or because somehow that particular architecture never engaged the culture?

PÉREZ-GÓMEZ:

That's another really complex problem: Mies and Mexico. One can certainly see a relationship between Mies's 1923 Brick Country House and many of the works of Barragán, and at that level there is a kind of profound spirituality of the simplicity of the exercise. I think in the case of Barragán, it's grasped intuitively rather than through any kind of theoretical understanding . . . but there is also a superficial understanding of Mies by Mexican architects. Industrialization is an issue in relation to this Miesian influence. You will always find that in Mexico, industrialization and particularly prefabrication are constrained by the *enormous* amount of labor that exists. So it's always economical to make things *in situ*. I don't know what the future will bring.

BURIAN:

It's interesting to think about the notion of prefabrication in Mexico as "trying to make water go uphill."

PÉREZ-GÓMEZ:

Another interesting issue follows from the implications of the architect as builder in Modern Mexican architecture. This relates to what I was saying about what to me is the greatest virtue of Mexican architecture: the crafts and the way things are put together and the knowledge of materials. Mexican architects tend to develop a tremendous expertise in putting things together; this, coupled with a greater "sweetness of the climate," often results in tremendous virtuosity. The results can be quite beautiful and exquisite, or absurd. This resolution of details is not at the level of the kind of mathematical precision of Scandinavian architecture; rather it's like *the presence of love in a rough object*. There is another level of Miesian influence related specifically to the Polytechnic tradition, which is reflected in the architecture school's alignment with the social agenda and pedagogy of Hannes Meyer.

BURIAN:
But not at the Universidad Nacional?

PÉREZ-GÓMEZ:
Mies's connection is mostly with the Polytechnic. Reinaldo Pérez Rayón, the architect of the huge campus of the Polytechnic in the north of Mexico, used IIT [Illinois Institute of Technology] as a model for the campus for the Polytechnic. While at IIT there is a kind of rationalization that has to do with the industrial base of the United States, in Mexico it becomes a formal device that is then carried out with conventional craftsmanship. In fact, it was complicated to modulate everything—I remember the module was 90 centimeters. Because there was no tradition of modular construction in Mexico, *everything* had to be ordered specifically for the campus. So there is a kind of contradiction where the connection with Mies becomes purely formal rather than related to the means of production, which was the interest of Mies at the time he designed IIT. I think that perhaps the Polytechnic is the greatest Miesian impact on Mexico in addition to his own Bacardi Building.

Félix Candela and Mexico

BURIAN:
Are the churches of Enrique de la Mora, in Monterrey and elsewhere in Mexico, and the buildings of the Catalan Félix Candela, uniquely Mexican in their conception, vision, feeling, or character? Are there, to use your terms, "mythopoetic narratives" or "symbolic order" in this work? Why does this work seem to have been embraced in Mexico and elsewhere in Latin America but virtually "jettisoned" from the larger discussion of modern architecture in the United States?

PÉREZ-GÓMEZ:
First, about Félix Candela, his work is certainly special. There are some fascinating details, particularly configurations of the general spaces under the shells. The problem I always had with Candela's structures is how they meet the ground. His hyperbolic parabolas became associated with gas stations, a truly pragmatic use of these concrete umbrellas. What is at stake here is to use forms that can be determined by simple equations of analytic

geometry. Thus the wooden form work can be constructed with straight lines. That is a kind of structural determinism. It might be poetic—one can say that Candela is poetic or that [Eugène-Emmanuel] Viollet-le-Duc is poetic—but the theoretical framework for the architectural form remains structural determinism.

BURIAN:
What about the work in relation to the tradition of Mexican Baroque architecture?

PÉREZ-GÓMEZ:
I don't think they are particularly "Mexican" buildings, and I don't think they respond to a Baroque legacy such as those complex spaces where you have a plastic integration of the mural and the space. They are virtuoso forms, sometimes well detailed and producing unusual effects. De la Mora's churches involve exquisite craft. There is, on the other hand, no questioning of the rituals in a way that postmodernity demands.

BURIAN:
Earlier you spoke about Le Corbusier's reformulation of the traditional Catholic program at the chapel at La Tourette. Could you explain that more fully?

1.10. Enrique de la Mora y Palomar and Félix Candela; Iglesia de San José Obrero (Church of St. Joseph the Worker), Monterrey, Nuevo León, 1959. Photo by Edward R. Burian.

PÉREZ-GÓMEZ:

At La Tourette, Le Corbusier takes a program that is given to him, to make a monastery for the Dominicans, and twists it so that we never find anything where we would have expected to find it; it's very simple, yet it's experientially very complex. These contradictions heighten the universal, "non-dogmatic" spirituality of this place. He consistently went beyond the originally intended program or the program he received from the client. It is at that point that there is an intervention at the level of program, at a level of poetic narrative. I don't see that happening with the work of either Candela or De la Mora; they seem to be making very adequate functional solutions to the Catholic ritual with interesting structural solutions, and that's fine. But I would care to make that differentiation.

BURIAN:

I believe you are saying that architecture requires a kind of cultural and poetic grounding for this extraordinary collective recognition to occur, and that there needs to be some kind of reinterpretation of the program that engages the user in spiritual, personal, and cultural ways that result in a narrative. That is an entirely inadequate way of summing it up . . .

PÉREZ-GÓMEZ:

Yes, it's a complicated conversation. We could discuss this for a long time, but the simple answer is that the project doesn't end with the forms. For the architect, the architectural project is a proposal for how we might live, taking what the client wishes and transforming it into a poetic vision of how we should live. This involves social, political, and metaphysical issues. I'm not naive on this point: I know that sometimes it's possible to do things, and sometimes it's not possible to do things. Sometimes you have stubborn clients, sometimes you don't. Every case is different. But I think that it is crucial to remember that this is very much a part of the architectural project constituting the temporal dimension of architectural meaning.

The 1950s and 1960s in Mexico

BURIAN:
What was your reaction to the actual realization of the major modern projects in Mexico during the late fifties and sixties, specifically, the University City; the large housing projects in Mexico City such as Nonoalco-Tlatelolco, Juárez, Miguel Alemán, and others; and the Olympic Games projects? What was the impact of these projects on a city with such rich architectural traditions as Mexico City?

PÉREZ-GÓMEZ:
This architecture was always perceived as *both* modern and national. Nobody would even dream of questioning these projects because their formal origins lie elsewhere. As I have already explained, that's not even an issue in Mexico.

BURIAN:
Several writers in the last three or four years have discussed Modern architecture as another kind of colonial phenomenon that was imposed on developing countries by others. Do you think that is not the case at all in Mexico?

PÉREZ-GÓMEZ:
One can always make such claims from the perspective of a critical theory concerned with differences. I don't think that's the way Mexican architects feel, though.

BURIAN:
There is also an attempt in many of those projects to create a national architecture by the inclusion of murals with Mexican content.

PÉREZ-GÓMEZ:
Yes, to make it possible for more people to identify with it. I think that in general those things work in Mexico. Mexicans

49

were particularly proud of the Olympic Games projects in 1968. I think there was a real will on the part of the government that once the Olympics were over, these buildings should become great social institutions. There was also a clear intention to project Mexico as a modern place and showcase it to the world.

BURIAN:
When you say "modern," do you mean in the sense of Mexico *joining* the developed world? Are you referring to the desire of Mexico to be a *part of* the avant-garde, or rather that through the Olympic Games projects, Mexico *is* the avant-garde?

PÉREZ-GÓMEZ:
I think there is a sense that Mexico partakes of the avant-garde, and there is always the question of being more fully developed—well, that's what modernity is all about. I think that Tlatelolco was quite controversial. Some people had [negative] reactions from the beginning. It was a huge urban renewal project, a scar on the urban fabric. Mexico City, though, because of its vitality, tended to heal very well. The media reaction was positive because the media was a branch of the government. This is barely changing now. One should remember that in Mexico the patron is the government, and that the patron and the architect are always responsible for the work. The architect is important, but the patron is crucial. In Mexico it's like that. How enlightened the patron is, is really one of the issues. In the case of the Olympic Games, the patron, the body that guided the whole operation under Ramírez Vázquez, was particularly enlightened.

Mexican Literature and Modern Mexican Architecture

BURIAN:
Do you think there were parallels between the development of "magical realism" in Mexican literature and similar developments in Mexican architecture?

PÉREZ-GÓMEZ:
Magical realism. I would like to know more about that. Do you think there is a connection?

BURIAN:
I think that it has been a lost opportunity. And I think it's one of the most important developments in Latin American and Mexican culture, and yet the only people I know of who seemed to be

interested in developing that idea were a number of expatriated Argentinians who were trying to make projects based on narratives. There was never that kind of complementary effort in Mexico, to my knowledge. I think the only other discussion I have had regarding this issue was with Carlos Fuentes. He mentioned literary texts that portrayed the quality of vernacular Baroque churches, with their very austere and abstract exterior severely contrasted with the dark space of the interior with its golden, luminous *retablo,* which produce the quality of a dreamlike experience . . .

PÉREZ-GÓMEZ:
That's a reading of the Baroque through the eyes of magical realism. But this is not magical realism in the sense of twentieth-century literature, programmatically connected to architecture.

BURIAN:
But even using that idea metaphorically was never utilized as a kind of spatial experience or as part of the design process.

PÉREZ-GÓMEZ:
The roots of modern architectural theory in Mexico in relation to literary theory . . . I don't think there was ever in Mexico a connection between architectural theory and literary and philosophical discourse. That's what I would argue. It's very disconnected. I don't think there has been an intellectual space to understand how important these relationships are. There is always this obsession with "theory," but it's instrumental, material that you can apply and that can get you on course. The humanities are generally lacking from modern architectural education in Mexico, although there may now be some exceptional programs with which I'm not familiar.

Postmodernity

and Mexico

BURIAN:
Do you think that Modern architecture has passed into history or that this discourse is still integrally related to the making of contemporary architecture in Mexico?

PÉREZ-GÓMEZ:
There have been some attempts to discuss this question of postmodernity in Mexico by some architectural writers. There is an awareness of discussions that happen elsewhere. I'm probably

not the best person to ask about the status of this conversation, having been away for many years now. Despite any rhetoric, it seems to me that the practice and the teaching of modern architecture is still within the parameters of modernity as I defined it earlier. Given the particular changes that probably will take place when Mexico becomes a more open democracy, I think there are changes that will first have to be acknowledged and assimilated on a cultural level and then will eventually manifest themselves in architectural conversations. I think that there is a kind of dislocation between aspirations and reality. Maybe an upgrading of the political system will start resolving the terrible social contradictions that still exist. I think that at that point, Mexico will be able to start having a meaningful discussion regarding the end of progress, the end of "History," in the sense of one large major narrative, and then I think there will be a possibility to "cast a line" back to tradition—not only to the kind of propagandistic reconstruction of the pre-Columbian tradition but also to colonial architecture in Mexico—to be able to translate into the present in a more self-conscious way some of the potentialities that were part of that world. So that's one aspect of it. The fact that somehow it becomes possible to believe that "human-generated change" is not all that matters, which is a concept philosophers working in different fields in Europe and North America are finally starting to digest. This is really about the end of striving for change for the sake of change, and it places novelty in architecture in a different light. The Modern movement was all about the new, the avant-garde was all about the new, and the new had value because it was new. Once one realizes that progress is a "construction," that things that really matter actually are not subject to this kind of development, something may start to change. But then there is the issue of the Mexican character. Can Mexicans live up to the personal honesty, responsibility, and respect for the other that may allow a truly postmodern society to function? This is not evident.

BURIAN:
Do you think that the average person shares this view?

PÉREZ-GÓMEZ:
The end of "progress," in Europe and North America? It is starting to happen. Yes . . . I think among young people, particularly. Young people are starting to feel that we're really not going anywhere . . . and it's part of the problem, part of the anxiety. In Mexico I think that in general you will find that that's not yet the

issue; we are always going somewhere. We are going to be like the United States. . . . And again, just to respond very simply, I think that while this may be happening in postindustrial cultures, it's hardly happening in Mexico, if happening at all. The obsession for progress is as present as it has ever been. It's a kind of utopia that marks and characterizes modernity. So to speak about these questions of the overcoming of technology, of somehow establishing a different relationship with our historicity, I think that those topics have very little bearing on the reality of Mexico at the present time.

BURIAN:
Monterrey is perhaps the most extreme example of that attitude.

PÉREZ-GÓMEZ:
To be able to engage in the discourse of postmodernity, and alternatives, one has to first start to feel at a popular level that that narrative, that History with a capital *H,* is wearing down. And you are right, it's not very clear in Europe and America either. Having said that, I think what might happen or might never happen in Mexico (i.e., its fall into postmodernity) would allow a reevaluation of the whole tradition of the culture in a way that would not be biased by any kind of instrumental mentality. Invaluable things that have remained buried because they were perceived to be archaic or absurd could be recovered and reintegrated into the present toward a richer future for all Mexicans.

BURIAN:
After novelty is seen in a new light, do you posit that more fundamental relationships to the body, the earth, or the sky above might develop?

PÉREZ-GÓMEZ:
Indeed, all the things that are really important. In this regard, Mexico has an advantage . . . because they are still important for the indigenous people.

BURIAN:
An exhibition recently initiated at Yale, entitled "South of the Border: Mexico in the American Imagination, 1914–1947," has traveled in the United States and Mexico. The show discussed and explored the phenomenon of Americans "discovering" Mexico between the World Wars. Several critical ideas were presented. One was the need for modern people in the United States

to connect with some kind of more "mythic" culture. For example, the show portrayed the admiration of the photographer Edward Weston and the anthropologist Frances Toor for the folkloric qualities of Mexico and what they perceived as the spiritual dimension of Mexican culture. The implication, although you don't directly state it, is that somehow Mexico has to leap beyond the need for progress . . .

PÉREZ-GÓMEZ:
I would like to believe that it could. But I don't know, it is a conjecture . . .

BURIAN:
Technical rationalism dominates many aspects of the contemporary Mexican culture . . . the notion that "if all Mexican schoolchildren had twenty megs of RAM on their desk, the nation will be inherently better for this." There is that sensibility, but there is also, and I may be completely wrong, a stronger sense of mythos, or mythic sensibility in Mexico . . . that the past is more present, the present more haunted. Even the connection to the family, as opposed to being primarily connected to your computer or TV screen, manifests this sensibility. The fact that one's allegiance is to the place where you came from, its people, your family . . .

PÉREZ-GÓMEZ:
I agree with you. I have complete sympathy for what you are saying . . . And yet, the belief in technology as the strongest possible value is also *overwhelming* in Mexico. It's overwhelming because it has been the program of the nation, particularly after the Revolution, and a most credible "front" for the deviousness of politicians and irresponsible administrators. So, it's anybody's bet. But I have complete sympathy with what you are saying, one could imagine that somehow all of this nonsense could be left behind and a reconnection could be found. But I have my profound doubts.

BURIAN:
Do you think [Rufino] Tamayo was getting at this? Tamayo was also profoundly criticized for not developing a national art, but in fact, I think he was exploring issues of what it is to be human.

PÉREZ-GÓMEZ:
Tamayo is indeed quite exceptional. I admire the muralists'

power, but Tamayo I really *like*. I think there is profound spiritual sense there, I agree with you. Politicians could learn much from the best (critical) Mexican artists and writers and take a position about technology not being a god, or that which has to be accomplished, but understand that it's a mode of "weak truth," as many other traditions have been. I think that then the retrieval of possibilities from the Mexican tradition would be feasible and the reconnection that I allude to might take place. Understanding artistic vision might also help weaken the chauvinism (not only in Mexico) that is the source of many problems. While the Mexican tradition would become one of many traditions—and these would obviously open the work to a more universal understanding—a reciprocity would start to operate, an understanding of the other by the Mexicans, and an understanding of the Mexicans by others, which would allow a much more healthy reconnection with its own internal tradition. For me, that is what is sadly needed.

1.11. *Helen Escobedo, Manuel Felegruez, Mathías Goeritz, Hersua, Sebastián, and Federico Silva; Espacio Escultero ("Space" Environmental Sculpture), Ciudad Universitaria (University City), Mexico City, 1976. Photo by Edward R. Burian.*

BURIAN:

In the United States and in many countries, I feel that the disconnection from a mythic past is like a limb that has been cut off. But in Mexico, I feel like it's a finger that was cut off; however, the nerves are still there and are still partially intact and their impulses are still traveling back and forth.

PÉREZ-GÓMEZ:

In the arts and in literature I think there is immediately greater possibility for this reconnection, for art transcending its boundaries if you like, leaving behind progress and this kind of grand Mexican History with a capital *H*. But in architecture it seems somehow more difficult. This has to do with a technological frame of mind and the fact that it's rather impossible to question the efficiency of parameters when one is involving practice. That seems to always be the issue, a more progressive architecture . . .

BURIAN:

The problems of nationalism, internationalism, and ideology are fascinating problems within post-Revolutionary Mexico. Octavio Paz pointed out these issues when he stated:

In Mexico, fortunately, we did not have a total ideology, an idea transformed by revolutionary ecclesiastics into a universal catechism, the foundation of state and society. . . . The absence of a revolutionary idea, however, was resented by many intellectuals in particular. Certain of them wanted to fill the vacuum, some, such as Vasconcelos, with philosophies and ideologies of global import. Among them, and in the first rank, Marxism, which in the twentieth century has been the ideology par-excellence of the intellectual class. . . . The revolution was more than a rectification of the vices and errors of the dictatorship. On the one hand, it was a resurrection: the Mexican past, Indian civilization, popular art, the buried spirituality of a people; on the other, in the juridical sense and in the figurative one of a thorough, ongoing beginning.

Do you have any comments or reactions to these statements?

PÉREZ-GÓMEZ:

It's true the Revolution had a sense of a resurrection of Indian civilization, and I think that what you would find in the history of architecture books regarding pre-Hispanic culture has to do precisely with that. What is the relevance of this tradition with the modern? Nobody ever talks about it, nobody touches the issue, it must be relevant, but we don't know how. It's an interesting problem. I think that Paz is right on that point. It's curious that the Revolution, with the end of the dictatorship of Díaz, also led to a severing of Mexican culture from developments in France and produced a vacuum, making us more vulnerable to this obsession with progress.

BURIAN:
What kind of cutting off are you talking about?

PÉREZ-GÓMEZ:
There were, for example, excellent Romantic writers in Mexico in the nineteenth century. In my view, the Revolution created a vacuum, and of course Paz can characterize this as an "ongoing beginning." And I like that idea. But what is the status of this ongoing beginning in the late twentieth century after part of the Revolution has been discredited? Perhaps that is what is at stake. That's why the political changes that will take place are of great importance. I think to truly evaluate the tradition, you have to demystify the official history, this kind of official line that has been construed as the History with a capital *H*. There has to be demystification in order to gain access to some more authentic and fascinating aspects of the tradition that one may bring back to the present. In the same way, though it sounds paradoxical, in order for Mexican architecture to prosper from that tradition, the official line has to be weakened. You know about this chauvinism, the Mexican that only looks inside for inspiration and doesn't want to acknowledge connections to other worlds. Tamayo was criticized for being an exception. So I think that is what is needed: weakening of this official line that has been so dominant in Mexico since the 1920s. Otherwise, we seem to always be driven by technological imperatives, more or less made palatable by formal devices and again more or less successful in terms of how they translate the spirituality of the culture. But the challenge becomes very important once the numerous workers crafting the concrete shells of Candela are no longer there, once the means of production are brought in line with those of postindustrial countries actually excluding the human hand from the making. At that point, if this weakening doesn't take place, the production of buildings in a place like Mexico would become an even greater abomination.

BURIAN:
Many people believe that the world would be a better place if everyone was instantaneously connected to electronic information systems, leaving us more time to . . .

PÉREZ-GÓMEZ:
And what are we going to be *doing,* right? Give us more time to do *what?* . . . I always ask myself! In any case, for the time being, technology is time-consuming. How much time do we have to waste keeping up with the latest gadget, with the latest software?

Conclusions

PÉREZ-GÓMEZ:
It's very hard to offer concluding remarks to a conversation like this. I guess a crucial issue that I think you raised is whether Mexico can avoid some of the absurd aspects of the technological development that seem self-evident in some advanced industrial societies. I'm not optimistic.

BURIAN:
You wonder whether the kind of life in Mexico City currently based on progress and technology as ends in themselves is really worth it?

PÉREZ-GÓMEZ:
I have the same sense as you about Mexican tradition, it's so *rich,* it's so earthbound. But when you actually go to Mexico City and you have twenty million people living in the most inhuman conditions, you wonder, is this tradition that I think is there, *really* there? The food, gestures, music, and dance are all in place, and yet, if the tradition were there, and if it mattered, *how is this possible?*

BURIAN:
Because everyone must be obsessed with progress in order to have an income to be able to consume products such as a car and a television?

PÉREZ-GÓMEZ:
Not only that, the conditions to accomplish very little are totally inhuman. I really don't get it. You could turn it around and say that what is operating here is a kind of negative paradise, a hell on earth or something.

BURIAN:
At some point will the system collapse?

PÉREZ-GÓMEZ:
I've been told this happens once in a while. Today it's completely unpredictable. You take your car, you never know, sometimes traffic just stops. When I left there in the seventies, everybody would get desperate, *upset!* Now—nothing! There is total resignation, it is almost *mystical,* this kind of reversal . . . it's *hard* for me to name what this might be. I would have to think much more about it, but it has a quality of, like you say, expiation . . . something that is necessary, a suffering that is somehow worth it, otherwise you wouldn't be there.

BURIAN:
Is the intellectual stimulation of living in the capital or the connection to your family worth it?

PÉREZ-GÓMEZ:
I don't know, to me it's a very fascinating question, particularly with regard to Mexico City. Mexico City is rich in many things; however, twenty million is about one quarter of the population of Mexico. One quarter of the population of the country lives in such circumstances for some purpose . . . what purpose? If somehow that hasn't struck home, when will it? To speak about postmodernity in a place like that seems almost impossible. It is the most modern place on earth, in that sense, and because it is the most modern place on earth, it's hell on earth, and it's enduring it. That's how I see it. It's really frightening. It is the extreme example of a mentality present throughout the "developing world."

BURIAN:
I believe the roots of this traditional culture are so strong that they literally "come through the cracks in the sidewalk." You can still find a place like the courtyard of the Museo Nacional de Antropología e Historia. It's interesting to think about. In much of your writing, you talk about reevaluating our current dilemma; for instance, in one of your essays you use John Hejduk's work as an example in which technological representation is utilized for poetic content.

PÉREZ-GÓMEZ:
The culture is present in personal interaction, just as in the con-

tradictory Mexican character. Hejduk's work, however, tends to *question* the use value of the technology, which is the only value that Mexico presently understands. It's very simple when you see it that way. The issue is to question the value of technology to demonstrate that it's not *the* value . . . not a strong value. It's hard to imagine that that is possible in a context like Mexico City. I don't think that Guadalajara and Monterrey are so far behind . . .

2

POLITICS AND ARCHITECTURAL LANGUAGE

Post-Revolutionary Regimes in Mexico and Their

Influence on Mexican Public Architecture, 1920–1952

Antonio E. Méndez-Vigatá

Introduction

Anyone who studies Mexican architecture will inevitably be fascinated by the diversity and quality of the architecture produced in Mexico during the thirty years that followed President Alvaro Obregón's (1920–1924) ascension to power. The sheer number of buildings constructed during the period was the result of the ambitious building programs undertaken by various post-Revolutionary regimes to satisfy the demand for new buildings, since little had been built during the years of armed revolution from 1910 to 1920, when virtually all economic activity was brought to a halt.

However, the diversity of architecture produced during this period was nothing short of amazing! Architecture was rapidly being produced in a variety of modes of composition. In fact, individual architects were simultaneously producing projects in varying architectural languages. Those languages, including neo-Colonial, neopre-Hispanic, and what has been termed the "International Modern," served as a vehicle to convey different ideologies and messages that each government in power was trying to project. Both the neo-Colonial and neopre-Hispanic were overtly nationalistic and expressed the will to portray a national identity in opposition to foreign influences. Thus, it was an approach aimed at preserving "traditional" Mexican culture and values. The International Modern was thought to project the modernness of the post-Revolutionary government and the hope of a new future, a future that would include Mexico among the most "progressive" nations in the world. This vision of the future would not only solve the injustice that precipitated the revolution in Mexico but also satisfy the needs of the peasantry and the emerging proletariat. In this sense, both approaches were highly utopian, one aiming at restoring an idealized past, the other aspiring to a future where machines, technology, and modernity itself would bring progress to the masses.

Previous commentaries on this era of Mexican architecture are vague in regard to the causes behind this diversity. The reticence to confront this issue can be attributed to politeness or even ideological complicity on the part of commentators and the desire to present an image of the country and its culture as a unified, post-Revolutionary culture well along the path to modernity. This vision of modernity could also be used to justify governmental policies as well as the demands for sacrifice placed on the masses.

The ideologies of succeeding governments during the period were as diverse as the various factions of the Revolutionary movement, sometimes contradictory, sometimes extremely simple and coherent. These governments have claimed their legitimacy by invoking the Revolution and even institutionalizing it. The PRI, the National Institutional Revolutionary Party, has been the channel through which this has been accomplished. The invocation of the Revolution as the genesis of modern Mexico has caused most historians to present a linear and monolithic view of Mexican history. This has resulted in the omission of nonclassifiable, eclectic buildings, and the identification of the post-Revolutionary period with *funcionalismo* (Functionalism).

Architecture was one of the many devices at the disposal of the government to form ideas. This was understood from the beginning, and one can draw a parallel evolution of architecture and politics in Mexico, the one reflecting the other. It has been claimed by some that the succession of governments in Mexico from 1920 until the 1980s followed a pendulum movement, going from left to right and then from right to left. The left began with Venustiano Carranza's government (1915–1920), which produced the current Mexican constitution. This was contradicted by the more moderate government of Alvaro Obregón (1920–1924), which again was contradicted by the more liberal government of Plutarco Elías Calles (1924–1928), and so on. According to the supporters of this argument, this political pendulum movement continued up to the Miguel de la Madrid presidency (1982–1988), when a neoliberal approach was adopted and continued by his successors.

This could also be said about architecture, which followed a pattern that went from the search for a national identity and its appropriate image to the portrayal of Mexico as part of the international avant-garde. This notion of the duality of post-Revolutionary culture has been discussed by Octavio Paz in *The Labyrinth of Solitude* in terms of the search for Mexico's past and the will to make it come alive in the present, and yet also the will to become "modern" and "insert" Mexico into the twentieth century.

Of course, the way to attain this was never considered in a monolithic way by the succession of post-Revolutionary governments. In fact, the Revolution encompassed the most diverse and contradictory ideas, from socialism to fascism, from nationalism to internationalism, from a will to uphold land reform and return to our agricultural past to the desire to industrialize our country. This diversity of agendas was able to ensure, until January 1994, a period of relative peace in Mexico.

The extremely varied political agendas of each succeeding administration are echoed by the diversity of architecture of the period. This production was divided between the public (government-sponsored buildings) and the private (domestic architecture and private enterprise). Most public architecture closely followed the ideology of each succeeding administration, while private architecture developed more autonomously, following the dictates of fashion and taste. This eventually resulted in an approach to architecture that was not only diverse but schizophrenic.

In this context, the focus of this essay is an examination of the various post-Revolutionary regimes in Mexico and their influence on the formation of culture, education, and the particular manifestation of architectural language in public architecture.

Architecture in Mexico during this period has been, as in the case of many regimes, at the service of the state. The role of the architect, however, was neither precisely stated by the government nor consciously accepted by the architects. The preferences of each government have always been expressed in Mexico through the assignment of projects to architects whose work was already known by government officials and who could be trusted to design buildings capable of conveying the desired image. Thus, it was more a matter of awarding projects to meet ideological goals than of dictating a set of rules of composition.

Architects involved in politics were eager to satisfy the demands of the government. Others, as in the case of Juan Legarreta, Alvaro Aburto, and Juan O'Gorman, out of social concern tried to improve the conditions of the working classes. Nonetheless, architects became, willingly or unwillingly, instruments at the disposal of the government.

The Ministry of Education and the Ideological State Apparatus

The political agenda usually expressed itself through the office of the Ministry of Education, which not only controlled elementary, secondary, and higher education in Mexico, but also "regulated" painting, drama, sculpture, and architecture through its Departamento de Bellas Artes [Department of Fine Arts].[1]

The Ministry of Education became a tool to preserve and disseminate the ideology of the government very much along the lines of what the French philosopher Louis Althusser has defined as an Ideological State Apparatus[2] or "a certain number of realities that present themselves as precise and specialized institutions[3] . . . which work *ideologically*, but also occasionally in a repressive manner, even though this happens only in extreme situations and manifests in a calculated and even symbolic manner."[4] The purpose of these Ideological State Apparatuses was to preserve the existing ideology through the "reproduction of its production conditions" and to disseminate, in the case of the school system, the necessary knowledge, attitudes, and norms of behavior—both civic and professional—to maintain the status quo.[5] In referring to the Educational Ideological State Apparatus, Althusser claims:

> But no other ideological State apparatus has the obligatory (and not least, free) audience of the totality of the children in the capitalist social formation, eight hours a day for five or six days out of seven.[6]

Education became one of the most important issues of the post-Revolutionary agenda of the Mexican government, not only to remain in power but also because the education of the masses had not really gone beyond the speeches of politicians and generals during the years of armed struggle in Mexico.

> The office of the president has dedicated, and shall continue to dedicate, a preferred attention to popular education. This is the most important and transcendental function of public power, the most noble of institutions of our time, and at the same time, the most fruitful to the social and economic well-being of our fellow citizens. This is not only for their moral and civic betterment. The greatest dispersion of popular education will make the reestablishment of the tyranny that has dishonored our history for so many years an impossibility.[7]

Thus, the Ministry of Education became one of the most dynamic branches of government, not only through the control of the educational system of Mexico and its Bellas Artes program, but also because it undertook *the most* ambitious construction program in Mexico from 1920 to 1952.

The Role of

Education in Post-

Revolutionary

Governments

In the 1920s (and even before that if one examines the Mexican Constitution of 1917), the issue of education was understood as vital by the post-Revolutionary government. Education exerted an influence that did not limit itself merely to educational issues, and it reflected the sometimes incongruent aims and diversity of the post-Revolutionary governments. The third article of the Mexican Constitution dealt with the issue of education and reflected the ideological issues and implications behind it. When the constitution was drafted in 1917, it made the separation of church and state definitive:

Education shall be free, it will be non-religious and taught by the State, the same as primary, elementary and higher that is given by private institutions. No corporation or religious group or minister of any cult may establish or become the principal of any primary school. *Primary schools can only be established under government supervision* [emphasis added]. Primary education in public schools shall be free.[8]

This article was the culmination of fifty years of liberal governments in Mexico that sought to diminish the influence of the Catholic church in our country. It was modified in October 1934, a few weeks before the presidency of Lázaro Cárdenas began, to become even more radical:

The education offered by the State *shall be socialist* and should exclude any religious doctrine, and fight fanaticism and prejudice. In order to attain this it shall organize its teaching and activities in such a way that it will create in the youth *a rational and precise concept of the universe and social life* [emphasis added].[9]

Of course, this amendment was the product of the conflict between the Catholic church and the state, but it also aimed, as Calles acknowledged in a rare insight into his ideas, to ideologically control the future of Mexico through its children and youth.

The revolution is not finished. It is necessary for us to enter a new period that I would name as a psychological revolutionary period: *we must enter and get hold of the conscience of children and the youth, because they are and have to belong to the revolution,* because the children and the young belong to the community, and the revolution should ban the prejudices and *form a new national soul* [emphasis added].[10]

This article was modified once again in 1946, at the end of the presidency of the nationalist and more right-wing government of President Avila Camacho:

The education offered by the national state—federation, states, and municipalities—*will tend to develop harmonically all the abilities of human beings* and will simultaneously encourage in the student the love for our country and the conscience of international solidarity of independence and justice. Under the warranty of the freedom of religious beliefs, as stated in Article 24, the criteria that shall inspire this education will maintain itself free from any religious doctrine, and based on the *results of scientific progress* will fight against ignorance and its effects, servitude, *fanaticism*, and prejudice [emphasis added].[11]

Vasconcelos and the Neo-Colonial Movement

José Vasconcelos's political and cultural agenda affected the image and production of architecture during the period in which he was minister of education (1920–1924). This image was the product of Vasconcelos's ideas on architecture, art, and culture, in which he was consciously trying to restore the golden age of New Spain, a time when he felt that the moral and cultural values of Mexico had been at their highest point. These ideas were intertwined with the Spanish American movement that opposed the hegemony and cultural dominance of Anglo-Saxon culture (i.e., the United States) that had been favored by most of the governments in Mexico since the War of Reform in the mid–nineteenth century. These governments copied the institutional models of the schools and universities of the United States, forgetting, according to Vasconcelos, that "Mexico had a University before Boston, and libraries, museums, newspapers and a theater before New York and Philadelphia."[12]

Since it was a movement that based itself on the idea of recovering criollo values through our "blood and language," there was little interest in the architecture produced outside of Latin America. This fact is evident when one examines the Mexican architectural periodicals of the day, where the only "modern" building of review was [Auguste] Perret's church at Raincy (published in the newspaper *Excélsior* on April 20, 1924, under an article entitled "Como deben ser nuestras iglesias" [How our churches should be], by Federico Mariscal), which reflected an interest that was probably more the result of its construction technique rather than its aesthetic innovation. Later in the 1920s, when Vasconcelos was no longer in government, a renewed interest in Modern architecture manifested itself. Many articles in both national and international magazines that were read by Mexican architects of the time featured buildings by Le Corbusier, Emil Fahrenkamp, Walter Gropius, J. J. P. Oud, and others.[13]

Government-sponsored architectural production during this period was extensive, as much needed to be done. The Alvaro Obregón regime (1920–1924) was actively trying to attract the badly needed foreign capital necessary to rebuild Mexico; thus, the government was eager to project an image of stability. Vasconcelos persuaded the Obregón regime to adopt neo-Colonial architecture and to favor a group of intellectuals that included the writers Pedro Henríquez, Alfonso Reyes, Martín Luis Guzmán, the philosopher Antonio Caso, and the painters Roberto Montenegro and Diego Rivera, among others. In architecture, the regime specially favored Carlos Obregón Santacilia, a great-grandson of Benito Juárez, who produced the most distinguished and important buildings of the period. But perhaps the greatest contribution of Vasconcelos to the political agenda of the government was his understanding of the role of education and the capacity of drama, sculpture, mural painting, and architecture to convey ideas to the masses. These ideas were mainly concerned with a return to a nostalgic, glorious past that he believed had existed in the colonial era:

To build is the duty of each epoch, and buildings shall be the glory of the new government. . . . We did not want schools of the Swiss type, like those that Justo Sierra [minister of education during the later years of the deposed Porfirio Díaz regime] hastily threw together, nor schools of the Chicago type [a criticism of O'Gorman's architecture], like some few that were perpetrated later. In architecture, too, we should find inspiration in our glorious past.[14]

Two of the most important works of the period were designed by Carlos Obregón Santacilia: the Escuela Benito Juárez (Benito Juárez School; 1923) in the neo-Colonial style and the Mexican Pavilion at the Rio de Janeiro Exhibition (1922). Both draw their inspiration from the colonial era and from Mexican Baroque religious architecture. But according to the government, one of the most important buildings of the period was the Estadio Nacional (National Stadium), the first important project designed by José Villagrán García, who later became the most revered academic theoretician of the Modern movement in Mexico. The Estadio Nacional was a stadium for 60,000 people, built with the intention of being the crowning achievement of the Bellas Artes (Fine Arts) branch of the Ministry of Education. But the program was not that of a simple sports arena. In fact, it was designed primar-

2.1. Enrique Aragón Echegaray, urban design; sculpture by Roberto Montenegro; Parque México and Colonia Hipodromo (Arcade in Mexico Park), Mexico City, 1927–1938. Photo by Edward R. Burian.

ily in terms of the acoustics requirements for public assembly, not merely for sporting activity. This was clearly the manifestation of architecture to consolidate the political agenda of the post-Revolutionary state.

We had lots of discussion then, and since, about the shape and size of the stadium. I refused to make it a mere race track. What I cared about above all was having an open-air theatre in which to give ballets and gymnastic events, and to present the choruses of different schools. Therefore, we made studies of the right proportions from the acoustical point of view, not just from the point of view of the rules of different sports. I preferred to have an open space in which the human voice would not be lost, rather than a bigger space in which amplifiers would be needed.[15]

In fact, all the presidential inaugurations from 1924 to 1934, with the exception of that of Abelardo Rodríguez in 1932, took place at the stadium, as well as most of the government political rallies of the period. This anticipated [Albert] Speer's Zeppelinfeld of 1934 as a political architectural artifact. Neither project was designed merely in relation to the requirements of sports; in reality both were open-air theaters to house performances that exalted national values and the health of the masses.

The Estadio Nacional was not accidentally sited in front of Obregón Santacilia's Escuela Benito Juárez. It had a simple horseshoe plan with a series of arcades that gave it an image similar to the generic *plaza de toros* (bullring) in Mexico. Because of its abstraction, it portrayed the image of a rather austere Roman building, an image that was perhaps more the result of economy

2.2. José Villagrán García, Estadio Nacional (National Stadium), Mexico City, 1929. Photo courtesy of the Archive of Louise Noelle Merles.

2.3. *Carlos Obregón Santacilia, Benito Juárez School, Mexico City, 1923–1925. Photo courtesy of the Archive of Louise Noelle Merles.*

than of an aesthetic preference but that expressed a will to transcend time.

At the end of Obregón's regime, when capital became more scarce, a less ornamented (and thus cheaper) version of neo-Colonial architecture came into favor. But the conflict of national identity that had just begun to be explored by intellectuals of the time, and the fact that the next president was a personal enemy of Vasconcelos, placed the "revolutionary" expression of government architecture back into the forefront. Thus, the issue of *mexicanidad* (Mexicanness) continued to be emphasized during the next two decades.[16] These inquiries explored the definition of "the Mexican" in relation to his past, creating a myth that draws upon many of the stereotypical characteristics of the Mexican from "popular" sources as opposed to the pressures that industrial capitalism was exerting on production.

This search was reflected not only in architecture and the arts. As pointed out by Roger Bartra, the government also adopted a "Janus-like" attitude that looked both at the past and the future, and sought to legitimize itself and the "new culture" it was promoting. *Both* the revival of the *ejido,* a colonial institution to advance land reform, *and* the pursuit of foreign capital for the industrialization of our country were policies that were simultaneously advanced. In a complex way, the government sought to create an image of national culture in which the masses would be able to recognize themselves.

Perhaps one of the major protagonists who most clearly reflected this phenomenon in his government-sponsored work was the muralist Diego Rivera. He simultaneously portrayed themes of country life and the industrial city. He praised the aesthetic values of popular folk art and advocated communist ideals, thus intertwining the myths of our past and future.

In music, a similar phenomenon occurred. Carlos Chávez, at the instigation of Diego Rivera, composed between 1926 and 1932 the suite *Caballos de Vapor* (Horsepower), in which the industrialized, mechanized, and consuming Northern Hemisphere (the United States) was contrasted with the Southern Hemisphere (Latin America) "full of forms, color, sunshine and exuberance."[17]

This contradictory approach created a sort of mimesis, similar to the condition that Erich Auerbach has described. A relationship between two events or entities could be realized outside the space and time frame of the moment;[18] in other words, the government was trying to legitimize itself by invoking both the mythic past and a utopian future. In this case, through this mimesis, a vertical structural connection between the government and the masses was created, a connection that converged in the state as creator of the myth of Mexican nationalism. The government was seeking ways to receive *political support* from the masses, and yet also sought to embody *the values* of the masses. Because the government had in its control the ideological apparatuses that could shape and transform the general populace, the masses began to reflect the values proposed by the government. Of course, this implied a separation between the state and the people, which has been responsible for many of the misfortunes we have endured in this century. As a result, history dissolved and the present was repressed, thus postponing the much-expected redemptive force of the Revolution to deliver a utopian future. As Minister of Education Moisés Sáenz stated in 1928:

Mexico has the right to have its own physiognomy. . . . A vigorous culture, a well-defined national soul will be the only thing that can save us from any kind of imperialism, and at the same time would be the most valuable contribution we may make to the advancement of humanity.[19]

Calles and the Political Agenda in Architecture

During the regime of President Plutarco Elías Calles (1924–1928)—which extended far beyond his presidency through the puppet presidencies of Emilio Portes Gil (1928–1930), Pascual Ortiz Rubio (1930–1932), Abelardo Rodríguez (1932–1934), and the first six months of Lázaro Cárdenas's term (1934–1940)—a succession of nine ministers of education took charge of the politics of culture in Mexico. José M. Puig Casauranc, minister of education from 1924 to 1928, and the Methodist Moisés Sáenz, minister of education in 1928, largely dismantled

Vasconcelos's cultural policies, but took advantage of the prestige and organization of the Ministry of Education for propaganda purposes. This fact becomes evident in the Mexican Mural movement if one analyzes Diego Rivera's, Jose Clemente Orozco's, and David Alfaro Siqueiros's paintings that became more politically controversial and critical regarding the Spanish origins of our culture from 1926 onward. In 1927 the Cristeros movement, a religiously inspired revolution that reacted against the anti-Catholic policies of the Calles government, emerged on the Mexican political landscape. As a result, what little remained of the aesthetic and cultural ideas of Vasconcelos in terms of the political agenda of the government was finally dropped in favor of either a more international, progressive, and "modern" image or a heavily decorated architecture inspired by pre-Hispanic motifs useful for propaganda purposes.

The Calles government was not the first in Mexico to sponsor buildings with neopre-Hispanic themes. In the 1920s, when the issue of national identity emerged again in Mexico's history, several architects and intellectuals decried neo-Colonial architecture as "foreign" or as an image from a submissive colonial era that was inappropriate to become the official architecture of an independent Mexico. Previous governments had already exhausted other styles, and the Calles regime (although not very discreetly supported by former President Obregón, who was already thinking about a second term) was trying hard to distance itself from Vasconcelos's aesthetic and political ideas. In this context, the period of neopre-Hispanic revival architecture asserted itself in Mexican architectural culture.

In 1926, Ángel Bachini designed the Casa del Pueblo in Mérida, a building that was the seat of the Partido Socialista del Sureste (a socialist party founded by Felipe Carrillo Puerto—who was murdered in 1924 for taking part in the de la Huerta uprising of 1923—that controlled Yucatan during the first five years of the 1920s). This building was designed according to Beaux Arts principles of symmetry, scale, and proportion. However, all its ornamentation was inspired by Mayan architecture, with the extensive utilization of Mayan arches to confer upon the building its pre-Hispanic character. This use of ornament to depict a national identity is not exclusive to this building, as similar attempts had been made by Adamo Boari at the Teatro Nacional (today, the Palacio de Bellas Artes) in Mexico City at the turn of the century.

Manuel Amábilis was a Paris-trained architect who had an

2.4. Diego Rivera, detail of The Exploited Mexican People *mural at the National Palace, Mexico City, 1935. Photo by Elena E. Abrahamsson B.*

eclectic approach to architecture, a trait shared by many Mexican architects of this period. He had a long career that spanned four decades and attempted, since the second decade of this century, to produce neopre-Hispanic architecture. In 1927 he was hired by the Calles government to design the Mexico Pavilion at the Iberoamerican Exhibition of 1929 in Seville. This building

*2.5. Manuel Amábilis,
Mexico Pavilion at the
Iberoamerican Exhi-
bition, Seville, Spain,
1929. Photo from
Manuel Amábilis,* El
pabellón de México
en la Exposición
Ibero-americana de
Sevilla, *Figure 6. Used
with permission.*

was a more serious effort to convey an image of pre-Hispanic architecture through the use of heavily ornamented surfaces. In
fact, its central plan was derived from the Nahuatl *nahui ollin*
symbol.

Yet all of these attempts fell short of achieving the aims of
their designers, since they were more or less superficial elabora-
tions of pre-Hispanic architecture that did not express the richness of pre-Hispanic space and did not follow as closely or
successfully the original models upon which it was based as was
the case in neo-Colonial architecture. This problem may have resulted not only from the lack of understanding of the architect
but also from the absence of any significant antecedents of pre-
Hispanic interior space. This search for the "pre-Hispanic" character would continue in the following decades, and as we shall
see, culminated in some respects with the design of the terracing
at the Ciudad Universitaria in the 1950s.

During the Calles government, Modern architecture in the International Style made its appearance in Mexico. The Granja
Sanitaria (Animal Laboratory; 1925) by José Villagrán García,
along with Carlos Obregón Santacilia's project for the School of
the Blind and Mute (1924), can be considered to be the first
buildings to be designed in an abstract modern language in Mexico. In fact, both buildings were designed while their architects
were still designing buildings in the neo-Colonial style. These
two projects marked a shift in the government-sponsored con-

struction (although some government officials still preferred for their own houses to be designed in the neo-Colonial style; for example, President Calles's house in Cuernavaca was designed in this style by Carlos Obregón Santacilia and Enrique del Moral).

Obregón Santacilia's school project is a bolder attempt at embracing International Modern architecture, since it departs from the use of symmetry and employs some ribbon windows. José Villagrán García's Granja Sanitaria was a more transitional project that looked similar to Garnier's Cité Industrielle project, with its use of cornices and eight-sided entrance arches. In fact, the mid-1920s for both these architects marked an extremely eclectic period during which they produced neo-Colonial, Modern, neo-Classical, and proto-Rationalist projects. How this was possible can be understood by examining the teaching system at the Academy of San Carlos, which closely followed the Beaux Arts model until the 1940s. Modern architecture was considered only another style, although its use was reserved for students in their last two years of course work.[20] This created a complex situation in which many architects tended to regard architecture merely as style, while the government saw it as image making and an ideological device. During the Maximato (so named because Calles was hailed by the press and members of the government as the "maximum chief of the Revolution"), when Calles controlled the political situation behind the presidencies of Emilio Portes Gil (1928–1930), Pascual Ortiz Rubio (1930–1932), Abelardo Rodríguez (1934), and the first six months of Lázaro Cárdenas, the state simultaneously favored neopre-Hispanic, International Modern, and even Art Deco architecture. However, International Modern architecture was seen by intellectuals within the government as a way of projecting the *modernness* and *progressiveness* of the Calles regime. Simultaneously, the state was attacking Catholic values and undertaking a large propaganda effort to project a new image of Mexico and its leader (who viewed himself as a "socialist") in newspapers and magazines in both the United States and Europe. Since the government believed that this architecture expressed its particular vision of modernity, architecture dropped overt references to the past or to Mexican culture that the government wanted to reform. Little by little it started to commission architects' buildings with less and less ornamentation, as Art Deco became less popular among left-wing circles, and began to favor, as we shall see, the more austere modern buildings and the functionalist architecture supported by Juan O'Gorman.

Villagrán and the Teaching of Theory of Architecture at the Escuela Nacional de Arquitectura

The Huipulco Tuberculosis Sanatorium of 1929, designed by José Villagrán, was a carefully programmed building that established Villagrán's career as a hospital designer. It still made use of axes of symmetry, cornices, and "punched" windows, but its abstract massing and strict functionality are thoroughly modern expressions. By 1934, in his Escuela Hogar Infantil (Children's Home School), Villagrán, in collaboration with Enrique de la Mora y Palomar, finally liberated his architecture from his previous rigid use of symmetry. This little-known work was one of his masterpieces, a dynamic building that responded to the site, took advantage of its orientation, and made use of natural sunlight.

José Villagrán, who was undoubtedly one of the most important architects practicing architecture during the period, was also the most eminent theorist of architecture in Mexico at the time, and he exerted an enormous influence on several generations of Mexican architects through his course on architectural theory at the National University.[21] This influence began to be felt soon after he started teaching in 1924.

Villagrán's theory of architecture has never been properly written. What has come to us, although revised by him, was nothing more than the notes taken by students during his classes,

a fact that makes the assessment of his ideas difficult for those who never had the opportunity to attend his courses.[22] An examination of these texts, prepared either in a very abridged form or posthumously with the care and love of former students, yields an extremely peculiar collection of ideas. One finds a hybrid mix of the architectural theories of Durand, Guadet, Reynaud, and Vitruvius, and some of Le Corbusier's writings intermingled with a preoccupation with the concepts of utility in architecture, aesthetic proportions, optical corrections, and a Ruskinian view regarding honesty of architecture. It seems clear that he was never able to escape his Beaux Arts training, a fact that becomes readily apparent when one examines his chapter on proportion and on optic corrections, or his analysis of architectural precedents in terms of axis of symmetry, polarity dominance, equilibrium, juxtaposition vs. composition, volumetric massing, etc. Of course, José Villagrán was a great advocate of Functionalism; however, his ideas were imbued with Guadet's views, especially when he considered the production of buildings as the creation of aesthetically pleasant objects by using proportional methods, and as the satisfaction of users' needs through well-defined architectural programming. Despite Villagrán's reliance on nineteenth-century French theorists,[23] he was able to arouse the interest of many of his students regarding the Modern movement. We do not really know whether this was the result of his teaching, his architectural practice, or the times. His former students eventually joined forces with him in developing the modern and functionalist languages of architectural composition in Mexico.

2.6. José Villagrán García, Tuberculosis Sanatorium, Huipulco, Mexico City, 1929. Photo courtesy of the Archive of Louise Noelle Merles.

Villagrán's complement to his theory, as in the case of any architect, is his practice, where one finds the same diversity apparent in his teachings. In the 1920s he designed, apparently without any qualms, neo-Colonial, Modern, and Mexican Art Deco buildings with the same skill.[24] Perhaps this was the result of his Academia de San Carlos student years, when he was trained as an architect in the Beaux Arts model, thus acquiring the capacity to compose in different modes.

O'Gorman and Bassols

Juan O'Gorman was a product of the Academia de San Carlos and had worked in the architectural office of Obregón Santacilia, where he collaborated in the design of the Escuela Benito Juárez. His later approach to architecture in the thirties was extremely influential in professional circles. O'Gorman was very critical of

2.7. Antonio Muñoz García, Centro Escolar Revolución (Central Primary School of the Revolution), Mexico City, 1933–1934. Photo courtesy of the Archive of Louise Noelle Merles.

the efforts made during Vasconcelos's tenure at the Ministry of Education. He felt that money had been wasted in the construction of pretentious buildings such as the Escuela Benito Juárez and the Estadio Nacional.[25] At this point in his career, he espoused that architecture had nothing to do with beauty or spirituality, and in 1933 he even stated that it should be "nonfanatical"[26] (a word that appeared [coincidentally?] in the Education Law of 1934) and international. His approach to architecture in the early 1930s had its roots in Le Corbusier's ideas and expressed a concern for functionality. He was placed in a very strategic position through his friendship with Narciso Bassols, minister of education from 1931 to 1934 under the presidencies of Pascual Ortiz Rubio and Abelardo Rodríguez. During this period O'Gorman built thirty primary schools in Mexico City for fifteen thousand students, a primary school in Tampico, and the Escuela Vocacional (Technical School) in Mexico City. His goal was the "maximum efficiency with the minimum expense of money and effort."[27] These buildings were among the best that were produced by the Modern movement of the thirties in Mexico, and they influenced many architects, including those belonging to the Liga de Escritores y Artistas Revolucionarios (LEAR; League of Revolutionary Writers and Artists) and the Unión de Arquitectos Socialistas [Socialist Architects Union].

Cárdenas and the Myth of the Modern

During the regime of Lázaro Cárdenas, functionalist Modern architecture became more entrenched, while at the same time a group of artists under the leadership of Diego Rivera and Juan O'Gorman began to explore ways in which some of the qualities

2.8. José Villagrán
García, National
Cardiology Institute,
Mexico City, 1937.
Photo courtesy of the
INBA, Dirección de
Arquitectura.

of the pre-Hispanic cultures could be incorporated into architecture. Although O'Gorman was investigating the use of some architectonic references to pre-Hispanic architecture, this did not hinder his ability to master the modern language in projects such as the Escuela Vocacional (Vocational School; 1932) or the Confederación de Trabajadores de México (CTM Project; 1934) or his Anteproyecto de Habitaciones Obreros (Preliminary Scheme for Federal District Workers Housing) in Mexico City from the early 1930s. At this time, most of the modern architects who later became successful in the 1940s and 1950s, such as Augusto H. Alvarez, Raúl Cacho, Enrique Yáñez, and others, were either completing their architectural training or just beginning to produce Modern architecture.

During this same period, Villagrán designed another hospital, this time one for which there was no precedent: the Instituto Nacional de Cardiología (National Cardiology Institute; 1937). This cardiac hospital took his language of Modern architecture a step further by the incorporation of a highly successful ramp system and a carefully studied circulation that linked the two asymmetrical volumes. One of these volumes contained all the restricted areas, and the other contained the beds and the more or less public spaces.

This building, currently being remodeled, was a milestone in Villagrán's career and was followed by other hospital projects. The Hospital Infantil (Children's Hospital) of 1939, a less-successful building that was initiated about five years earlier following another architect's design, utilized symmetry and incorporated a Mendelsohnian aesthetic similar to the one Villagrán had employed at the Escuela Hogar Infantil of 1934. Unfor-

2.9. Carlos Greenham, detail of facade, Main Hospital of the National Railroads of Mexico, 1936. Photo courtesy of the Archive of Louise Noelle Merles.

2.10. Carlos Greenham, Main Hospital of the National Railroads of Mexico, 1936. Photo courtesy of the Giffords Collection.

tunately, this earlier building developed structural problems while still under construction. Villagrán was called in at a late stage, but the problems were never satisfactorily solved and it was finally demolished in 1957. However, this building was not unique to the period. Carlos Greenham's Hospital General de Ferrocarriles (National Railroads Hospital; 1936) also utilized this design sensibility, and featured a taut, streamlined facade that alluded to movement by utilizing motifs from ships and airplanes.

National Identity and Architecture during the Avila Camacho Regime

In 1940, General Manuel Avila Camacho succeeded Cárdenas as president in an election that was tainted by electoral fraud. The government of Avila Camacho was preoccupied with the possibility of being dragged into World War II (which eventually became a reality in May 1942), and aspired to form a National Unity government aimed at harmonizing the different political forces in Mexico. This program of Acercamiento Nacional was launched with a symbolic public event, designed to project an image of reconciliation, in which Avila Camacho appeared together with all the living former presidents. The truth of the matter was that they were not on good terms among themselves. This event, along with many other actions, created the myth of National Unity under the leadership of the new president, who had also declared during his political campaign that he was a Catholic. This fact is extremely important, because no president had made such a declaration since the War of Reform (1858–1861). This brought peace of mind to most of the middle class that had been scandalized by the left-wing anti-Catholic position of the government during the preceding presidencies of Calles, Portes Gil, Ortiz Rubio, Abelardo Rodríguez, and Lázaro Cárdenas.

During Avila Camacho's regime, the Ministry of Education attacked illiteracy and continued the school construction effort that had been initiated almost two decades earlier. Avila Camacho also founded the Instituto Mexicano del Seguro Social (IMSS; Mexican Social Security Institute), created to solve the social security needs of the working classes. This resulted in an enormous construction effort to provide health services over all of Mexico. In Mexico City, the IMSS headquarters was designed in 1940 by Carlos Obregón Santacilia in a thoroughly modern manner using the largest glass facade built in Mexico at that time.

It is also important to note that from 1944 until 1945 Hannes Meyer was in charge of the Comisión de Planeación de Hospitales (Hospital Planning Commission), a body that established the requirements for hospitals in Mexico. (Meyer was the director of the Bauhaus in Germany from 1928 to 1930, and worked in the Soviet Union as a school designer and town planner from 1930 to 1936.) Under his administration, many hospitals were constructed, the most important of which was the Hospital de la Raza (1945) by Enrique Yáñez, a building that served as a model for many others built in Mexico. But perhaps the most important construction effort made during the Avila Camacho regime was the school construction program undertaken by the Comité Administrador del Programa Federal Construcción de Escuelas (CAPFCE; Administrative Committee for the Federal School Construction Program), a body in which Hannes Meyer also played a role as coordinator from 1945 to 1947.[28] The aims of this government body were, in the words of then–Minister of Education Jaime Torres Bodet, "to build schools, and when we build them, we shall never forget that true luxury in a school is not in the use of marble or bronze but in the *combined utility of all its parts, the articulation of all its sections, the consequent exercise of its function*"[29] (emphasis added). In fact, the CAPFCE was a public entity that allowed private construction companies to assist in the construction of schools under the supervision of the government. The CAPFCE defined the image that the new schools had to project, suggesting that the buildings had to *adapt* to the *geophysical* and *social* conditions of each region and at the same time be *modern,* while the building methods of each region should be employed and the material used should be left exposed. Thus, the intention was to produce what some have termed a "critical regional architecture" that was both international and local.[30] In order to achieve this goal, many of the best architects of the period were asked to contribute primary school projects. José Villagrán García designed a school at the Colonia Garza in Tacubaya (1944), the Escuela Rancho del Rosario in rural Mexico (1944–1945), and the República de Costa Rica school in Mexico City (1945). Mauricio Campos designed a school in China, Nuevo León (1944–1946); Enrique del Moral also contributed with a rural primary school in Yuriria (1944–1946); José Luis Cuevas was responsible for the design of the Escuela de las Artes del Libro in Mexico City (1944–1946), while Pedro Ramírez Vázquez began his career by designing many rural schools in the southeast of Mexico. All these primary school buildings employed local materials and labor and were able to convey a modern image through the use of ribbon windows and, where climate and materials permitted, flat roofs.

This effort was highly influential in the subsequent design of school architecture, not only at the primary level but also at the secondary and university levels. The same aesthetic concerns and preference for a rational use of building materials were evident in other schools of the period built by other governmental bodies and by private enterprise. Buildings such as Vladimir Kaspé's Escuela Alberto Einstein (1944–1946), and even Mario Pani's Conservatorio Nacional de Música (1946) and Escuela Normal de Maestros (designed with Enrique Yáñez in 1945), were designed by a new generation of architects that became very successful during the next decade. It was this generation, in fact, that was largely responsible for the image of Modern architecture in Mexico City.

During this period, the explorations in the use of pre-Hispanic motifs in architecture were almost completely abandoned in government-sponsored work. At most, some of the ornamentation in public buildings included some pre-Hispanic motifs. Probably the only government-sponsored building of any importance that drew its inspiration from pre-Hispanic architecture was the 1940 Monumento a la Raza (Monument to the People), a pyramid built by Luis Lelo. But some architects, such as Mario Pani, had already shown a keen interest in these issues, as in the case of the Escuela Nacional de Maestros (National Teachers School; 1945), where an abstract mural dealing with *mestizaje,* by José Clemente Orozco, was placed in its courtyard as a focal point.

This interest eventually resulted in *integración plástica,* an approach that sought to integrate architecture, painting, and sculpture into a unified work of art. This aspiration resulted in the construction of the new Ciudad Universitaria under the government of Miguel Alemán (1946–1952). Not only did the murals move from interior spaces to exterior ones, appearing almost like billboards on the facades—even completely covering some of them—but the actual urban design of the campus, in terms of terracing and scale, took its inspiration from some pre-Hispanic principles. At last, the two aspirations of the 1930s, of expressing *modernness* and *Mexicanness,* were reconciled through the use of murals and urban design. This project was designed with the intention of reflecting the values of national identity as derived from the pre-Hispanic past, and applied them in buildings that made use of both modern materials and composition principles.

Conclusions

The openness of youth was also one of the attributes that Mexican architects conferred upon the architecture of the period. For example, Obregón Santacilia's most important works were produced when he was between twenty-six and forty; Villagrán's Tuberculosis Sanatorium was designed when he was twenty-eight; O'Gorman's architectural career started at age twenty-two, and he executed his best functionalist work while in his thirties. In fact, all of the important architects of the period were at the height of their careers between the ages of twenty-six and forty! Thus, the diversity of the period may also have been a result of a personal search by designers who were still young enough to explore modes of composition in which they could express themselves, and who had no qualms about changing their vocabularies in order to discover their identity and make an architecture appropriate for the time.

As we have seen, architectural production in Mexico between 1920 and 1946 was primarily at the service of government. Its diversity was, to a great extent, neither the result of it being autonomous nor a consequence of a lack of control. Rather, it had more to do with the diversity of ideas and approaches that were part of the Revolution. As Octavio Paz wrote in his book *The Labyrinth of Solitude:*

The Revolution began as a discovery of our own selves and a return to our origins; later it became a search and an abortive attempt at a synthesis; finally, since it was unable to assimilate our tradition and to offer us a new and workable plan, it became a compromise. The Revolution has not been capable of organizing its explosive values into a world view, and the Mexican intelligentsia has not been able to resolve the conflict between the insufficiencies of our tradition and our need and desire for universality.[31]

This also took place in regard to architecture. The image of our architecture became more homogeneous as the dominant ideology began to be homogeneous as well. Thus, Mexican architecture became more unified during the 1950s. In many respects, the issues surrounding *mexicanidad,* as portrayed in Orozco's mural on *mestizaje* at the Escuela Nacional de Maestros, proved to be prophetic. The new Mexican architecture was thought to be a mix of the modern and pre-Hispanic modes of composition. Our full and complete entrance into modernity could not be realized until the myth of our identity became more or less resolved. In this way, we could keep the values of our *mexicanidad* without the fear of losing ourselves in the modern (foreign?) world.

2.11. *Enrique del Moral and Mario Pani; Rector's Tower, with murals by David Alfaro Siqueiros, Ciudad Universitaria (University City), Mexico City, 1950–1952. Photo by Edward R.Burian.*

Roger Bartra, in his book *The Cage of Melancholy,* argues that Mexicans live between two worlds. His description reflects the complex nuances of modern Mexican culture, both the embracing of an exhilarating utopia and the introspection of a haunted mythic past.

This image of an amphibian culture [i.e., a culture that exists in two worlds], which must never decline into self-denigrating mimicry or extreme nationalism, is, from the middle of the twentieth century, offered as a role model; it has the additional attraction of permitting the Mexican to peer out of the abyss of the existential drama and feel the vertigo of the modern age.[32]

The diversity of architecture in Mexico from the twenties through the forties was in part a result of external factors that affected architectural production, such as new technologies, the social goals and ideological agenda of the post-Revolutionary state, and the economic pressures exerted by capital on the profession. This diversity was also a result of the internal dilemma that Antonio Caso, the Mexican philosopher and president of UNAM from 1920 to 1923, revealed in his book *El problema de México y la ideología nacional:*

One of our national characteristics is the fact that we have not solved the problem of the adaptation of two human groups with diverse cultures. . . . How can a people be formed with two such dissimilar cultures? How can we realize a collective soul with such heterogeneous factors? In the end, how can we create a congruous whole out of the incongruity of the conquest?[33]

Anyone who has visited Mexico has undoubtedly been struck by the fact that there are many Mexicos . . . many different cultures and modes of living . . . and many different ways of thinking and visualizing our identity at the same time and the same place. This has accounted for many of the political problems and cultural ambiguities that have characterized our history, since a unified project for a country never existed. The indigenous has often clashed with the occidental aspects of our culture. However, the lack of a coherent, unified view of ourselves has not hindered our desire for one. In order to satisfy this longing, we have utilized the devices at our disposal to create the illusion of a single, coherent, and unified Mexican culture, including ideology, politics, historiography, and the production of art and architecture.

As a discipline, architecture reinstated itself in Mexico during the period and legitimized itself through its alliance with the state. While the state commissioned many buildings by a group of young architects, architecture as a profession failed to affect society as a whole, since in terms of the total number of buildings, relatively few are, and were, designed by architects. In fact, most of what is built in Mexico are vernacular dwellings, informally built by their occupants, using materials and techniques readily at hand. The reality of most government-sponsored building is ultimately symbolic, rather than dramatically solving the overwhelming social needs of the nation. In spite of a number of well-intentioned projects to address the housing problem in Mexico, such as Mario Pani's Unidad Habitacional Miguel Alemán (Miguel Alemán Housing Project; 1948), their impact was minimal because of the relatively small number of housing units actually constructed and their relatively high cost for most workers. Ultimately, the limits of economics and a dominant state ideology prevented these efforts from benefiting the anonymous masses that instigated and endured the hardships of the Revolution. The ambition of attaining a collective identity and tangibly expressing it through architecture still prevails (every government in Mexico since the 1920s has had a favored architectural project), yet the influence of these projects on the built environment is still as limited and intranscendent as ever.

Notes

1. Curiously, the archaeological sites in Mexico were not controlled at the time by the Ministry of Education. They were under the care of the Ministry of *Agriculture!* Perhaps this was the reason, among others, that the minister of education under José Vasconcelos never really manifested interest in the pre-Hispanic past of Mexico.

2. L. Althusser, "Ideology and Ideological State Apparatuses," in *Essays on Ideology*, p. 136. In fact, Althusser included the school system and the cultural branches of government among the Ideological State Apparatuses. The idea that architecture is related to ideology and political discourse and is capable of conveying messages and ideas has been tacitly or openly accepted by architects and politicians for centuries. In late eighteenth- and early nineteenth-century architecture, French architects favored the *architecture parlante*. In the twentieth century, Adolf Hitler stated in 1929 that "out of our new ideology and our political will to power, we will create stone documents" (B. M. Lane, *Architecture and Politics in Germany, 1918–1945*, p. 107). In 1938, Hitler went on to say that "each great epoch expresses itself through its buildings. When people live in great times, they show their feelings. Their words are more powerful than their thoughts. This is the word in stone" (January 22, 1938, speech by Hitler, quoted by P. Adam in *Art of the Third Reich*, p. 229).

3. L. Althusser, "Ideology and Ideological State Apparatuses" in *Essays on Ideology*, p. 136. Althusser mentioned the Religious Ideological State Apparatus, the School Ideological State Apparatus, the Familial Ideological State Apparatus, the Judiciary Ideological State Apparatus, the Political Ideological State Apparatus, the Unions Ideological State Apparatus, the Information Ideological State Apparatus, and the Cultural Ideological State Apparatus.

4. Ibid., p. 138.

5. Ibid., pp. 126–127.

6. Ibid., p. 148. Francesco dal Co, in his chapter "Nationalistic and Totalitarian Architecture in Italy and Germany" in M. Tafuri's and F. dal Co's *Modern Architecture*, pp. 281–301, appears to utilize the concept of Ideological State Apparatus to examine Italian fascist architecture. Other books that examine the relationship of politics and architecture are B. M. Lane's *Architecture and*

Politics in Germany, 1918–1945 and L. Domenech's *Arquitectura de siempre: Los años 40 en España.*

7. See SEP, *La educación pública en México,* p. 211. Information about the exact number of schools is confusing, but apparently 1,159 new schools and 455 libraries were built between 1921 and 1922. During Miguel Alemán's presidency, 5,069 new schools were built. This effort is also reflected in the percentage of the national budget assigned to the Ministry of Education, which increased from 12,296,000 pesos (4.9% of the national budget) in 1921, to 427,773,000 pesos (10.7% of the national budget) in 1952. José María Puig Casauranc, minister of education from 1924 to 1928, claimed that he increased the number of rural schools from 960, the number when he took office, to 5,000, when he finished his tenure. For further information, see his book *El sentido social del proceso histórico de México,* p. 165.

8. See the Mexican Constitution of 1917.

9. In Mexico, the congress has the right to amend the constitution, which it did in this case.

10. Excerpt from a speech given by Calles on July 20, 1934, in E. Krauze, *Plutarco E. Calles,* p. 124.

11. Amendment by Congress of Mexico in 1946.

12. J. Vasconcelos, *A Mexican Ulysses: An Autobiography,* Part 3, "The Disaster," p. 160.

13. For more on the formation of Modern architecture in Mexico through articles in magazines and newspapers, see E. X. de Anda, *La arquitectura de la Revolución Mexicana* and E. Yáñez, *Arquitectura: Teoría, diseño, contexto,* p. 175.

14. J. Vasconcelos, *A Mexican Ulysses,* p. 181.

15. Ibid., pp. 187–188.

16. For a further discussion of this issue, see R. Bartra, *The Cage of Melancholy: Identity and Metamorphosis in the Mexican Character,* in which he explores the relationship between the intellectuals and the definition of the "Mexican" in this century.

17. From the notes by Carlos Bustillo on the record sleeve of Carlos Chavez's *Caballos de Vapor,* London Symphony Orchestra conducted by Eduardo Mata, RCA Records MRS-024.

18. E. Auerbach, *Mimesis: The Representation of Reality in Western Literature,* pp. 44 and 66.

19. M. Sáenz, *México íntegro,* p. 263.

20. This information was offered by Vladimir Kaspé, who studied at both the École de Beaux Arts in Paris in the 1930s and the Academy of San Carlos in the 1940s.

21. One must remember that the only school of architecture operating in Mexico until the establishment of the Escuela Superior de Ingeniería in 1932 was the Academy of San Carlos, currently the National School of Architecture at the UNAM.

22. Through the efforts of some of his former disciples, especially Ramón Vargas Salguero, most of the ideas of José Villagrán García have been published in four interesting books: J. Villagrán García, ed., *Teoría de la arquitectura* (INBA/SEP, 1964); V. Jiménez, ed., *José Villagrán* (INBA, 1986); R. Vargas Salguero, ed., *Teoría de la arquitectura* (UNAM, 1988); and J. Villagrán García, *Teoría de la arquitectura mexicana* (ASINEA, *n.d.*).

23. The most quoted one was Julien Guadet.

24. Of course, he was not the only architect who had such flexibility. Le Corbusier designed some neovernacular houses in northern France. In Mexico, Obregón Santacilia also utilized several modes of composition.

25. In a speech given at the 1933 debate organized by the Sociedad de Arquitectos Mexicanos, reproduced in R. López Rangel, *La modernidad arquitectónica mexicana: 1900–1940,* p. 209.

26. Ibid., pp. 188–203.

27. I. Rodríguez Prampolini, *La palabra de Juan O'Gorman,* p. 200.

28. Hannes Meyer's activities in Mexico have been analyzed by Jorge Gamberos Garibi in "Hannes Meyer: Su etapa en México," in *La arquitectura mexicana del siglo XX,* pp. 86–93.

29. Fragment of a speech given on July 10, 1944, by Jaime Torres Bodet at the laying of the first stone of the first school made by the CAPFCE.

30. For more information regarding the government's efforts in the CAPFCE programs, see Víctor Jiménez's essay "CAPFCE: 40 años de arquitectura," in *El Museo Nacional de Arquitectura.*

31. O. Paz, *The Labyrinth of Solitude,* p. 168.

32. R. Bartra, *The Cage of Melancholy,* p. 94.

33. A. Caso, *El problema de México y la ideología nacional,* p. 13.

3

MODERNITY IN MEXICO

The Case of the Ciudad Universitaria

Celia Ester Arredondo Zambrano

He knew that temple was the place that his invincible purpose required . . .
he knew that his immediate obligation was the dream.

—Jorge Luis Borges, "The Circular Ruins"[1]

Modernity, more than a period of time or an architectural style, was a deep-rooted belief in the power of architecture and the conviction that Modern architecture could transform society.[2] Modernity would produce a new environment that would create an ideal man. This ideal man, like the dream man described by Jorge Luis Borges in his short story "The Circular Ruins," wasn't the product of an everyday dream. He had been so carefully crafted and passionately desired that he magically came to life and became real.

International modernity and Mexican modernity, although both inspired by the need to create a new man, had different versions of what that ideal man might be. International modernity's ideal man was a universal man with one identity and one spirit. Mexico, on the other hand, conceived a man that would bridge the nation's contrasts and differences through a new national identity. Even though the conceptions of these two men are not the same, in both cases their power would be such that it would transform their world and their society.

Borges describes the genesis of a dream man as the product of the long painful labor of a magician who reached the circular ruins of an old temple and recognized it as the appropriate place to create his dream. According to this tale, there are two essential elements that must be present in this magical event, time (*chronos*) and place (*topos*). Mexican modernity, in its quest for the ideal man, had to achieve the adequate combination of these two elements. Post-Revolutionary Mexico offered the appropriate time frame that could generate the need. Now, a place, a circular ruin, was needed to evoke the dream and give it life. This mythical place was the Ciudad Universitaria [University City].

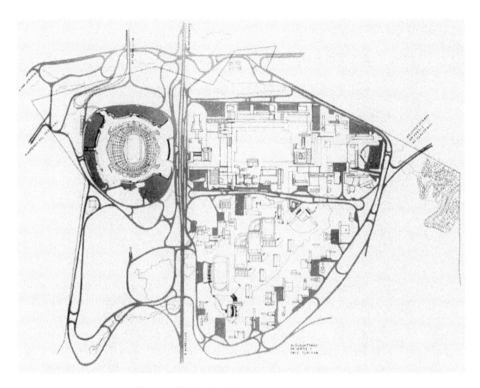

*3.1. Enrique del Moral and Mario Pani; site plan for the Ciudad Universitaria,
Mexico City, 1950–1952. Photo courtesy of the UNAM, drawing previously
published in Juan B. Artigas,* La Ciudad Universitaria de 1954: Un recorrido a
cuarenta años de su inauguración. *Used with permission.*

II

The Ciudad Universitaria was the mythical *topos* for the creation
of the new Mexican. It was the environment where a modern society would be born; therefore, it had to represent its ideals and
aspirations. Its architecture represented the Mexican contradiction of attempting to be modern while representing a national
identity.

The phenomenon of modernity in Mexico was determined by
the circumstances of the time and by Mexico's particular characteristics as a nation. This is in direct contradiction with the principles and doctrine of the Modern movement, which endorsed an
eternally present and international architecture, analogous to the
timelessness and universality of Classicism. Nevertheless, this contradiction was not apparent at the time, since both modernity
and Mexico shared the same dream.

To understand modernity in Mexico it is crucial to understand
this contradiction. Mexico took the ideal of a new man from

European modernity. European modernity, born after the First World War, envisioned a man that would unite all nations. This universality was viewed as a means to obtain international unity and peace in an environment where no national, ethnic, or social differences would be apparent.[3] Modern aesthetics and Functionalism seemed the ideal representation of that environment.

Post-Revolutionary Mexico needed to create a new man that would reunite all Mexicans into one nation, in an attempt to reconcile its own abysmal differences and contradictions. Mexico, longing for unity, welcomed the idea of a new man and a new environment and even embraced the aesthetic language of modernity. However, it did not long for an *international* unity but for its unity as a nation. Mexico's dream man represented the paradox of being both modern and Mexican, both international and national.

Nationalism was the solution to the dilemma, since it was viewed as a continuation of the revolutionary process through which social, economic, and political difficulties would disappear. It also represented the economic development needed to achieve international stature. As Roger Bartra explains:

The nationalism unleashed by the Mexican Revolution . . . holds that the wheels of progress and history have begun rolling toward a future of national well-being.[4]

This nationalism allowed the nation to remain Mexican while accepting wholeheartedly the notion of progress. Mexican modernity became synonymous with nationalism, and the dream of the universal man was replaced by a dream man that represented this national identity.

III   The void felt after the Revolution in terms of unity and national identity generated an imperative need to create the image of a new Mexican that would accomplish social change. Mexico's intellectuals knew the time was right, and like the magician in Borges's story, they searched for the appropriate place. In this case, the ideal place had to be created, and architecture played an important role in this task, responding to the modernist notion that believed in the power of the built environment to transform social behavior.

The Ciudad Universitaria, or CU as it is known, represented this perfect *topos*, the site where a new Mexican identity would be born. Constructed between 1950 and 1952, the CU was the product of a collaboration of a team of over 150 architects, engineers, and landscape architects, led by Mario Pani and Enrique del Moral.[5] Besides being the place for some of the most important examples of Modern architecture in Mexico, it was also the mythical place where dreams would turn into reality. The importance and significance of the Ciudad Universitaria as part of Mexico's history and destiny was passionately expressed in a speech by Carlos Lazo, director and general administrator of the project, in the ceremony for the laying of the first stone of the CU in 1950:

Mexico, a geographic crossroads, has been historically possible thanks to the collaboration of diverse forces and cultures. . . . Mexico has been built stone by stone. . . . And this [CU] is one of them. This is a moment for Mexico. In this same site where the Nahuas and Olmecas met in the Valley of Mexico, in the pyramid of Cuicuilco, the most ancient culture of the continent appeared from the contemplation of this land and this sky. We are building a University in its most ample sense, integrating the thought, the hope and the labor of all, through culture. We are not laying the first stone of the first building of Ciudad Universitaria, we are laying one more stone in the fervent construction of our Mexico.[6]

CU represented a tribute to Mexico's past and a promise toward its future. Its importance was to be always linked with its past and its national vocation. The mythical connection between past and present established by Lazo in his discourse was also part of CU's historical origin.

CU was constructed on the lava-covered ruins of Cuicuilco, a pre-Hispanic city dating from approximately 600 B.C.[7] This impressive site, which included lava formations and exotic landscape, was abruptly abandoned during the eruption of the volcano Xitle, between 300 and 200 B.C. According to legend, its people vowed to return to reinstate the lost culture with a new and stronger one. Although CU was a new built environment, it was nevertheless sited so as not to destroy its only surviving temple.

This decision to site the university in relation to the ruins of Cuicuilco reminds us of Borges's magician and his return to the circular ruins in search of their mythical power. This same power can be attributed to Cuicuilco, since its legend was united with modern and national ideals in an attempt to produce the return and the restitution of its lost culture.

Although CU was created *ex novo*, it was not created *ex nihilo*. Its newness was interwoven with the historicity of the site,

3.2. *Enrique del Moral and Mario Pani; aerial view of the Ciudad Universitaria (University City), Mexico City, 1950–1952. Photo courtesy of the UNAM, previously published in Juan B. Artigas,* La Ciudad Universitaria de 1954: Un recorrido a cuarenta años de su inauguración. *Used with permission.*

demonstrating the nature of Mexican modernity and the possible coexistence of opposites. By analyzing CU's built form and design concepts, it is possible to establish this paradox in its role of creating the new Mexican.

IV   The urban composition of CU, in contrast with its mythical origins, responds to the principles of modern urbanism. The super block, the separation of circulation systems, and the zoning of activities determined the site strategy of the campus. This strategy is closely related to the functional-determinist aspects of the modern city, but it was much different from Mies van der Rohe's scheme for the ITT [Illinois Institute of Technology] campus, in which the buildings were placed within a highly rational, determined grid. But like ITT, CU was built as, and still remains, an isolated portion of the city for the exclusive use of pedestrians.

The campus was divided into four parts by its road system. The main campus, located to the north, contains all the schools and their facilities. The sport facilities were to the south, while the Olympic Stadium and the dormitories were to the west and east, respectively.

The first scheme for the campus responded to rational-functional organizational principles. Common activities were centralized and expressed according to their function, which would be available to every school. However, the final scheme responded to the traditional strategy of organizing each school in its own individual buildings. Pedro Ramírez Vázquez criticized this arrangement[8] when he stated that it was as if the old schools scattered in the center of Mexico City were only relocated to this new campus. The buildings themselves were designed as freestanding elements by an interdisciplinary group of architects, engineers, and artists. The functional integration of the buildings presented a problem due to the site's uneven terrain. This was resolved by the use of walkways, grand staircases, and terracing reminiscent of pre-Hispanic architecture. On the other hand, the modernist aesthetics utilized in the composition of each building gave unity to the complex.

Modernist principles and historical references are interwoven in the design and conception of CU. The main campus, for example, has a certain regularity to it provided by a central axis and a great plaza. Yet it avoids being symmetrical by the interlocking arrangement of its buildings, alternating mass and void, along the periphery of the scheme. Although these characteristics are modern, the composition of the main campus is also similar to some pre-Hispanic cities. Its central axis resembles the Calzada de Los Muertos [Way of the Dead] at Teotihuacán in the sense that it axially steps up the site, while its great plaza reminds us of the plaza carved into the mountaintop at Monte Albán. In fact, CU bears a great resemblance to Monte Albán, since in both cases the composition is that of an asymmetrical equilibrium achieved by the relationship between built form and open spaces.[9]

Rational and mythical concepts seem to merge in the site design of the campus. The disposition of the main buildings located on the great plaza and central axis responds to both their functional and symbolic importance. The Rector's Tower (Mario Pani, Enrique del Moral, Salvador Ortega Flores) is set on the highest, most predominant part of the campus, close to the main highway, and acts as a gateway and welcoming element in the composition. The Main Library (Juan O'Gorman, Gustavo M. Saavedra,

Juan Martínez Velasco), with its multicolored mural by Juan O'Gorman, depicts Mexico's past and present wisdom available to the new Mexican. The School of Science (Raúl Cacho, Eugenio Peschard, Félix Sánchez Baylón) with its mural, located in the center of the scheme, represents the evolution of scientific knowledge that is available for Mexico's development. This organization reveals that even though the campus was inspired in relationship to a modern city, a symbolic arrangement seems to prevail in the composition.

3.3. Enrique del Moral and Mario Pani; Rector's Tower, Ciudad Universitaria, Mexico City, 1950–1952. Photo by Elena E. Abrahamsson B.

The buildings of the CU, although abiding by the tenets of the International Style, also reveal local idiosyncrasies and formal contradictions. Nevertheless, it is in the design of these individual buildings that the modern language is eloquently used, demonstrating the knowledge and comprehension of modern aesthetics and compositional principles. Enrique Yáñez gives an insight into this understanding of Modern architecture when he states: "Design the modest, the useful and the economic and from these characteristics obtain beauty . . . "[10]

This is a modern interpretation of the Vitruvian components of architecture: *firmitas, utilitas, venustas.*[11] Juan O'Gorman was also aware of this academic interpretation of the Modern movement when in 1968 he stated:

3.4. Vladimir Kaspé, Humanities Building, Ciudad Universitaria (University City), Mexico City, 1950–1952. Photo by Elena E. Abrahamsson B.

According to my judgment, it is indisputable that during this time, Mexico has established a new Academy of modern architecture as obtuse and closed as was the old Academy of San Carlos, constituted in the manner of the so-called Classicism of the School of Beaux Arts of Paris.[12]

3.5. Roberto Alvarez Espinosa, Pedro Ramírez Vázquez, Ramón Torres, and Héctor Velázquez, with mural by Francisco Eppens; La Facultad de Medicina (Department of Medicine), Ciudad Universitaria (University City), Mexico City, 1950–1952. Photo by Edward R. Burian.

Clearly the modernist style was interpreted as a new formal order. Hence, the buildings, in their proportions and regularity, responded to modern compositional principles[13] that emphasized form and volume. This was demonstrated by the expression of single volumes, such as the Main Library, or articulated volumes, such as the School of Medicine (Roberto Álvarez Espinosa, Pedro Ramírez Vázquez, Ramón Torres, Héctor Velázquez). These volumes are also organized in an asymmetrical manner, such as that which occurred in the Rector's Tower facades. Horizontality was not only sought as a modern aesthetic; it was also exaggerated as a formal and technical feat, as is evident in the Humanities Building (Vladimir Kaspé).

Functions are organized and fully expressed within the structural grid of each building. Floor plans are composed to articulate the rational distribution of the programmatic functions, which in turn are expressed on the facades. Modern materials, such as glass, concrete, glass block, and breeze block, are used to define and emphasize volume, structure, and functions.

By the same token, this interpretation of modernity manifested in the buildings is also evident in the urban design scheme. Even though the buildings and the site design respond to modern dictates, they do not seem to be created as part of the modern urban vision as in Le Corbusier's garden city. The open spaces are not really gardens or parks; they are plazas or walkways, which not only link each building but also have a symbolic meaning and a sense of place. The buildings, although conceived as autonomous elements, do not relate to their surroundings as in a modern city, where horizontal windows and corridors allow for a visual integration with the garden and the horizon. Horizontality is not viewed as an integration between interior and exterior as expressed by Le Corbusier's *fenetre longuer*, nor was it meant to streamline the buildings and their "silhouette against the sky."[14]

3.6. Enrique Yáñez, Enrique Guerrero, and Guillermo Rossell; Escuela Ciencias Químicas (School of Chemical Sciences), Ciudad Universitaria (University City), Mexico City, 1950–1952. Photo by Edward R. Burian.

It is not my intention to question the theoretical knowledge or design ability of modern Mexican architects. On the contrary, I wish to establish the need they had to respond to their *topos* and *chronos* and the commitment they felt in creating the dream man, the new Mexican, through the design and construction of the CU. To accomplish this task, it was necessary to simultaneously embrace inherent contradictions, such as the rational aspects of the Modern movement and the emotive qualities of the new Mexican dream man, through aesthetic and even mythical values. This struggle between function and emotion is the main dichotomy of Modern architecture, and according to O'Gorman, is impossible to solve, as he expressed in the following statement:

This problem will never be resolved by the [Modern] architecture. The contradiction persists related to the function of utility and the function of emotion or aesthetics.[15]

In spite of these contradictions, CU remained within the tenets of the International Style. The unorthodox elements used seem to appear in a rather unconscious and almost naive manner. I believe that the architects of the campus were aware of their mission to create an architecture for a Mexico that simultaneously looked to the past and future, while utilizing the language of the Modern movement to create a coherent vocabulary for the campus. There is no real attempt to create a unique, personal "signature architecture," except for perhaps the Cosmic Ray Laboratory by [Jorge González] Reyna. CU strived to endorse modernity as a way of life and also as the new Mexican identity. Yet, by using the language of Functionalism—a language that denies nationalism—it faced the difficulty of expressing a national identity. Nothing could be more inherently contradictory than the desire to express a national spirit through an autonomous architecture that attempts to liberate itself from social, cultural, and political references and achieve meaning in its own right, responding only to its own inherent values.

In spite of this contradiction, or perhaps because of it, the unstable mixture of Functionalism and nationalism was necessary to produce the new national identity. Mexican characteristics were linked to modern ones in an attempt to make modernity authentically Mexican. This was not the first place or time where this was done. When Walter Gropius first arrived in England, he appealed to the theories of [John] Ruskin and [Henry] Cole in an attempt to make modernity British.[16] In Mexico's case, the

3.7. Raúl Cacho, Eugenio Peschard, and Félix Sánchez Baylón, with mural La Conquista de la Energía by José Chávez Morado; auditorium, Science Complex, Ciudad Universitaria (University City), Mexico City, 1950–1952. Photo by Elena E. Abrahamsson B.

Bauhaus principle of *gesamtkunstwerk* was utilized in order to achieve this authenticity. The integration of artists, artisans, and architects proclaimed by the Bauhaus was the logical way in Mexico of introducing the nation's spirit and cultural values through the participation of its artists.[17] This became an objective at CU, where architects and artists were called on to form part of an interdisciplinary design team. It was through this collaborative effort that modern and national values would successfully unite, remaining faithful to both.

Unfortunately, this artistic integration did not mature into a theoretical or conceptual approach, and the participation of the artists was limited to the creation of murals on the blank walls allocated by the architects for this purpose.[18] The theme of each mural expressed the mission of each school and its educational intent. Murals were previously used in modern buildings by [Reinhard] Baumeister and [Amadée] L'Ozentfant, as discussed by Hitchcock and Johnson.[19] These artists used an abstract language that harmonized with the abstraction of Modern architecture. Mexican artists, on the other hand, preoccupied with the didactic aspects of the Revolution and Mexico's historical past, transgressed the International Style by resorting to murals that were representational, metaphoric, and symbolic. The murals, like those of ancient times, graphically depicted a cultural message.[20] Although heavily criticized and ridiculed (particularly by Bruno Zevi, who referred to them as *"grottesco messicano"*[21]), they served an important social and aesthetic purpose.

Besides the controversial murals at CU, there are two other exceptional buildings on the campus that were more successful in expressing national values. These are the *frontones* (Alberto T. Arai) and the Olympic Stadium (Augusto Pérez Palacios, Jorge Bravo, Raúl Salinas). During an interview, Ramírez Vázquez stated that both of these buildings have accomplished an exceptional historical and contextual integration. The *frontones*, or handball courts, are the most important elements in the sport area at CU. They were designed to mimic the neighboring hills of the Sierra de las Calderas located to the east. The intention was to create a sense of perspective by placing each *frontón* on a different plane. Alberto T. Arai eloquently integrated both technical and tectonic elements. He used a concrete structure of columns and slabs to support walls made of volcanic rock that are wider on the base than on the top, giving the appearance of the ancient pyramids.

The stadium's design has also been praised for its harmony with the site and its original construction and tectonic system. The height of the structure was diminished by creating a slope on the periphery, similar to [Tony] Garnier's Olympic stadium at Lyon. Ramírez Vázquez has inadvertently suggested that the stadium has a mythical origin, for he believes its shape implies that it has always been there. He feels that the site cannot be conceived without it being there, and that the slopes, with their cladding of volcanic stone, appear very Mexican.

The project of the CU is one of the largest projects of social content in Mexico, and many intellectuals, such as Carlos Lazo, considered it one of the most important manifestations of Mexican modernity. But for others, such as Ernesto Ríos González, who considered it "a sad example of decoration and integration,"[22] or Manuel Rosen Morrison, who called it "architecture of State, of propaganda and of national exaltation,"[23] the CU may not be the project that best illustrates the success of modernity in Mexico; they would probably have chosen buildings that closely resemble the international models of that time. In spite of this, the CU illustrates the struggles and shortcomings of the International Style in producing both an emotional and functional, as well as a traditional and modern, architecture according to the

3.8. *Jorge González Reyna and Félix Candela; Cosmic Ray Laboratory, Ciudad Universitaria (University City), Mexico City, 1952. Photo courtesy of the Archive of Louise Noelle Merles.*

dream man the architects wished to create. Perhaps CU's most important accomplishment was that it truly accepted the challenge of building an ideal environment where a new man and nation would be born. It valiantly expressed this mission in spite of its contradictions and, at times, in spite of the architects themselves. In the CU it is possible to see Mexican modernity and humankind's faith in architecture become a physical, social, and cultural reality.

V   Mexican modernity is not real for us anymore, because we do not share the same dream. It belongs to another time and place. Yet it was real enough to produce a new nation, a new concept of space for human activity, and our present reality was created and influenced by that vision of modernity.

Borges's magician, at the end of the tale, realizes in horror that he, like his dream man, is only an illusion and a dream that someone has dreamt. We Mexicans may also be surprised by our true identity. When we understand that we are only a product of someone else's imagination, the realization that we are only a dream may produce anxiety and confusion at first. However, later we may feel liberated to take life less seriously or we may reach a sense of awareness that may allow us to understand our limitations and responsibilities. In any case, we, like the dream that gave us life, have the responsibility of dreaming a new, alternative existence, part of a never-ending cycle of invented dreams, in which modernity played only a part.

Notes

1. "The Circular Ruins" in *Fictions* (New York: Limited Editions Club, 1984); Spanish edition: Borges, J. L. Borges, "Las ruinas circulares," in *Ficciones* (Buenos Aires: Emece Editores, 1956; Mexico City: Alianza Editorial, 1991), p. 62.

2. M. Tafuri and F. dal Co, *History of World Architecture I*, p. 113. The avant-garde movements like German Expressionism or Holland's De Stijl believed in the transformation of society through architecture and the built environment. This was certainly true for architects like Paul Scheerbart and Bruno Taut, since both believed that glass architecture had the power to transform humanity into "a super mankind dedicated, through love for its own inner freedom, to a symbolic fusion between culture and nature."

3. U. Conrads, *Programs and Manifestoes on 20th-Century Architecture*, p. 39. The transformation of the world into a united society through architecture was viewed, by the De Stijl movement in particular, as the ideal solution for humanity. As they explained in their Manifesto I of 1918, they desired to destroy the old ways of the "domination of individualism," and turn toward the universal by the "international unity in life, art and culture."

4. R. Bartra, *The Cage of Melancholy: Identity and Metamorphosis in the Mexican Character*, p. 114.

5. For further background regarding the evolution of the scheme for the campus, see the essay on the stadium of the CU that follows in this volume.

6. C. Lazo, "Piedra sobre piedra" in *Pensamiento y destino de la Ciudad Universitaria de México: 1952*, pp. 5–7.

7. P. Gendrop, *Arte prehispánico en Mesoamérica*, p. 37. Gendrop described Cuicuilco as one of the oldest pre-Hispanic pyramids, faced in stone with a circular plan composed by truncated conical elements in four stepped levels, which supports the formal relationship I have established between Cuicuilco and the circular ruins of Borges's tale.

8. The statements about CU made by Pedro Ramírez Vázquez that are cited in this essay were obtained through a personal interview he granted me at his office in the Pedregal de San Angel in Mexico City on March 24, 1994.

9. P. Gendrop, *Arte prehispánico en Mesoamérica*, pp. 124–125. Paul Gendrop describes Monte Albán's urban design using quotes from Holmes, Paul Westheim, and Raúl Flores Guerrero, which could appear to refer to CU's urban design if one didn't know beforehand what they were talking about. Flores

Guerrero's statement about Monte Albán's "display of asymmetrical harmony" could easily be interpreted as CU's main characteristic.

10. E. Yáñez, "Enrique Yáñez" in *Arquitectura*, p. 91.

11. M. Vitruvio Polión, *Los diez libros de arquitectura*, p. 14.

12. J. O'Gorman, "El desarrollo de la arquitectura mexicana en los últimos treinta años" in *Arquitectura*, p. 51. This was a special issue that commemorated the magazine's first thirty years.

13. E. Yáñez, *Del funcionalismo al post-racionalismo*, pp. 118–119. Yáñez does not give a full description of CU's buildings; instead he establishes the main elements that are present in their design, such as the rational methodology of Villagrán García and the notable influence of Corbusian syntax.

14. Le Corbusier, *The City of Tomorrow*, p. 232.

15. J. O'Gorman, "El desarrollo de la arquitectura mexicana en los últimos treinta años," p. 49.

16. L. Benevolo, *Historia de la arquitectura moderna*, p. 645.

17. F. Bullrich, *New Directions in Latin American Architecture*, p. 28. Bullrich discusses Mexican architecture and its search for a national expression that was interpreted as the integration of the arts or *gesamtkunstwerk*. According to Bullrich, Mexican architects believed this integration to be Mexican because it was also present in pre-Columbian and Mexican Baroque architecture.

18. M. Pani and E. del Moral, *La construcción de la Ciudad Universitaria del Pedregal*, pp. 96–97. Pani and del Moral include a description of all the murals at CU along with several quotes from their artists. The famous muralist Diego Rivera discusses his experience in the sculpture/painting of the Olympic Stadium as an integration between himself and the laborers, stonelayers, and bricklayers—in short, all the "eighty human sensibilities" involved in the task. The theory of the *gesamtkunstwerk* appears to have been accomplished in this mural, although this phenomenon was not experienced in all the other buildings at CU, as was expected.

19. H. R. Hitchcock and P. Johnson, *The International Style*, p. 73.

20. M. Pani and E. del Moral, *La construcción de la Ciudad Universitaria del Pedregal*, pp. 102–103. [José] Chávez Morado, the creator of the three murals of the School of Science at CU, explains the evolution undergone by Mexican muralism, which, according to him, reached a second stage at CU. He states that social and physical changes in both formal and technical aspects were accomplished. According to him, the murals in their formal aspects were more abstract and more related to the exterior of the buildings and their architecture, while in their technical aspects, the murals on the exterior had developed more resistance against the weathering of their materials. It is interesting to see through this statement how Chávez Morado was preoccupied in establishing the mural not as an ornament but as an evolved artistic manifestation of the modern vocabulary. Unfortunately, these ideas were not as convincing in the murals themselves, which were too Mexican and Baroque, as Bruno Zevi later claimed.

21. B. Zevi, "Grottesco Messicano" in *L'Espresso*, p. 16; also published in the Italian magazine *L'Archittectura-Cronache e Storia*, Rome, 1957, and republished and translated in the article "Crítica de ideas arquitectónicas" in *Arquitectura*, pp. 110–111.

22. E. Ríos González, in a response to Zevi's article; "Crítica de ideas arquitectónicas" in *Arquitectura*, pp. 113–114.

23. M. Rosen Morrison, in a response to Zevi's article; "Crítica de ideas arquitectónicas" in *Arquitectura*.

4   ARCHITECTURE AND PLACE

The Stadium of the University City

Alberto Kalach

Translated by José Carlos Fernández and Edward R. Burian

The Modern movement in Mexico emerged from the final years of the 1920s; however, it existed without a modern urban design intervention until the construction of the University City (Ciudad Universitaria, or CU). The University City was the first example of the principles of the Modern movement applied to a problem at the urban scale.

The site plan strategy of the CU had its origins in a competition initiated by the UNAM (Universidad Nacional Autónoma de México). The winning entry was derived from an earlier scheme

4.1. Augusto Pérez Palacios, Jorge Bravo, and Raúl Salinas; aerial view of Olympic Stadium, Ciudad Universitaria (University City), Mexico City, 1950–1952. Photo courtesy of the Archive of Louise Noelle Merles.

developed by three students, Teodoro González de León, Armando Franco, and Enrique Molinar, which Mario Pani and Enrique del Moral later adopted. The site plan and the specific proposals for each building were further developed by more than 150 architects and engineers. In spite of the fact that they worked in different groups, they were able to achieve a complex work of great aesthetic unity, as all were immersed in the tenets of the International Style, which marked an important moment in Mexican architecture.

From a historical perspective, we understand that what characterized the architecture of the CU was a power and spirit that went beyond an architectural style or the language of the avant-garde. The architecture of the CU revealed the hidden powers of place, landscape, and history. The essential site elements of the CU—the topography, vegetation, and microclimate of the place—were formed with the explosion of the volcano Xitle.[1] The utilization of the resulting great platform of volcanic rock in the terracing of the CU complex, the extensive use of this material for construction, and the tectonic logic—all conferred on the architecture its essential local character.

An important antecedent, usually forgotten in discussions of the CU, were the gardens of Pedregal by Luis Barragán. The photographer Armando Salas Portugal described these gardens as "the encounter between the sensibility of man before the dramatic presence of lava,"[2] thereby transforming our understanding of this landscape. This "inhospitable" zone was abandoned for centuries and was discovered by Barragán and transformed into one of the most exclusive subdivisions of the era. The spirit

4.2. View of stadium seating, Olympic Stadium. Photo courtesy of the Archive of Louise Noelle Merles.

and the beauty of the place, including its topography, vegetation, and distinct vistas, were revealed by Barragán.

Salas Portugal has also characterized El Pedregal as a "volcanic paradise or telluric gardens."[3] Barragán selectively intervened on this memorable site characterized by indigenous vegetation over a sea of lava. The addition of plazas and high walls constructed from the same stone, cultivated gardens, geometric reservoirs, and steel grids established a contrast between the natural and humanmade environments.

The plan for the urbanization of the Pedregal of San Angel created by Barragán included ordinances for the urban image. Extremely large, secluded private properties were created behind endless walls that were constructed from the volcanic stone from the site. This created a sense of unity, both for the public realm and the private gardens, and served to protect existing lava rock and indigenous vegetation on the site. These provisions, which were, unfortunately, later violated by others, sought to achieve a balance between nature and built form.

The gardens of El Pedregal were a direct source of inspiration for the landscape of the CU. Luis Barragán was invited to participate in the projects of forestation and garden design for the urban design directed by Pedro Ramírez Vázquez and Augusto Pérez Palacios, who was also responsible for the stadium project.[4] Although it is difficult to know to what extent Barragán participated in the landscape design for the CU, the gardens of El Pedregal set the tone and the formal vocabulary for the landscape strategy at the CU.

Making an analogy between modern urban space and pre-Hispanic ceremonial space may at first seem problematic. However, the CU presents us with a dual set of intentions. The treatment of volcanic stone, the construction, the terraces, plazas, monumental stairs, and sloping walls were conceived as a transformation of the original topography. This architecture of stone, understood as transformed topography, organized the urban space with great power and clarity. On the other hand, the modern, light, transparent buildings with their elegant and dynamic proportions were composed of glass, steel, concrete, and ceramic tile and were raised on pilotis. Thus, they were superimposed on and tectonically contrasted with an architecture that engaged the earth and the landscape.

This dichotomy produced a dual reading of the space. The elements of this lightweight architecture were overlaid on the sculptured platforms carved into the earth, which accentuated the dominance of the platforms. However, on occasions this lightweight architecture stands in contrast to the fluidity of the topographical space, thereby creating a secondary reading of greater complexity.

The Olympic Stadium at the western terminus of the principle axis in the composition of the CU is the most clear synthesis of this idea. The architectural chronicles of Luis de Cervantes describe the initial explorations for the stadium project, and how they derived general principles for many of the buildings, conferring on them a strong relationship to place.[5] The architects of the stadium, Augusto Pérez Palacios, Raúl Salinas, and Jorge Bravo, generated its conceptual ideas based on the understanding of the specific site (landscape) and the acknowledgment of the limited resources to realize its construction (technology). Out of these considerations, the project began to assume its own character.

The early schemes of the great stadium, designed to seat approximately 110,000 spectators, were conceived as a structure of reinforced concrete. However, this proved costly and strained the capacity of the Mexican concrete industry of the time. Other solutions were tried and eliminated until an inspired solution that clarified the tectonic and construction logic appeared. "The architects, in an attempt to escape their preconceived notions and to acknowledge a profound sense of place, opted for a unique and original solution."[6] They adopted a system of construction based on stepped terraces. *Tepetate* extracted from the center of the crater was methodically deposited to compose great terrace steps to access the stadium seats.[7] The exterior cladding of the sculpted mound also utilized the local volcanic stone.

This marvelous topographic intervention created by man suggests an architecture whose strength resides in the power of a conceptual idea and its relation to a place. The absolute correspondence between space, structure, and function surpasses any notion of style, while only a few accents in the stadium leave a trace of the epoch.

The pictorial and sculptural works of Diego Rivera that were suspended and never completed were intended to provide an ornamental surface for the exterior portion of the crater. Ultimately this was fortunate, as the purity and abstraction of a timeless work of architecture would have been lost.

All of the circulation of the stadium was resolved by means of ramps that were developed by cutting into the sloping portion of the mound (reminiscent of *taludes*)[8] or through it by means of tunnels that terminated at the center of the crater. In a real sense,

4.3. Exterior view, Olympic Stadium.

4.4. Exterior view of Olympic Stadium looking north from Rector's Tower. Photos by Edward R. Burian.

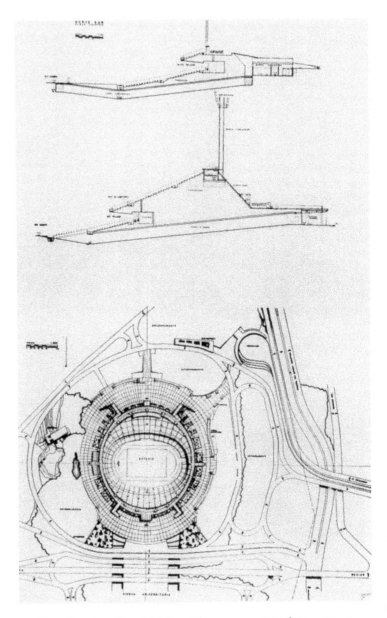

4.5. Plan and sections, Olympic Stadium. Photo courtesy of the Archive of Louise Noelle Merles.

4.6. Stadium lights at perimeter, Olympic Stadium. Photo by Edward R. Burian.

these elements were also conceived as part of the topography. The only other elements of the composition were the eight juxtaposed, lightweight sculptural pieces of architecture that were distinctly attached to the crater and conceived within the strict confines of rationality. These included the pressbox, the six (originally four) towers of illumination, and the scoreboard of the stadium. Together with the mural by Diego Rivera, these were counterpoints in this work in both tectonic and symbolic terms and established a symbol for its time.

The CU stadium should be understood, apart from its functional purpose, as a piece of landscape and urban design. Its siting is significant in terms of its position within the CU complex as well as the entire city. This topographic intervention is the culmination not only of the main axis of the CU but also of one of the most important north-south axes in the city, Avenida Insurgentes.

The power of conviction of the conception, in formal and tectonic terms, gives the stadium a sense of having always been there. Its architectural presence is so pregnant that it goes beyond time or fashion. This landscape architecture recalls the silent and archaic permanence of the pre-Hispanic era, yet it also has the rational spirit of Modern architecture.

The volcanic stone connects the architecture to the geologic time of Xitle; the concrete steel and glass present an architecture at the end of the millennium. The power of the space dislocates time and creates a place where past and future are present.

Notes

1. The volcano Xitle had several explosions in different periods before and after the establishment of Cuicuilco. The last recorded was in approximately 70 B.C.
2. For further information, see A. Salas Portugal, *Barragán: Photographs of the Architecture of Luis Barragán.*
3. Ibid.
4. For further information, see L. Cervantes, *Crónica arquitectónica prehispánica, colonial, contemporánea.*
5. Ibid.
6. Ibid.
7. Ibid. *Tepetate*, also known as *tezontle*, is a generic volcanic stone from the Valley of Mexico.
8. A *talud* is the sloping portion of the profile edge of a platform used to compose pyramids in a variety of pre-Columbian cultures in Mexico.

"THE GENERAL AND THE LOCAL"

Enrique del Moral's Own House, Calle Francisco

Ramírez 5, Mexico City, 1948

William J. R. Curtis

Art is universal, the accent is local.

—*Rufino Tamayo*

Much has been written about the intellectual prejudices of the early historians of Modern architecture, about their supposed determinism, and about their tendency to think of history in terms of an oversimple, linear development. But not enough has been done to unravel the geographical and cultural biases underlying the same narratives. Grand abstractions such as the "International Style" never did enough to acknowledge the ideological range and regional nuances of Modern architecture in the originating countries; but once instated, they were certainly guilty of overlooking the complexity of a dissemination that gained momentum in the 1930s, and that already witnessed a species of "cross-fertilization" between certain core concepts of Modernism, and interpretations of diverse national cultures, climates, and traditions.[1] One has only to think of works of the mid- to late 1930s, such as those by Erich Mendelsohn in Palestine, Oscar Niemeyer in Brazil, Sedad Eldem in Turkey, José Luis Sert in Spain, Junzo Sakakura in Japan, or Alvar Aalto in Finland, to be reminded of the richness of responses to a variety of "local" situations.

None of this is to deny the formative role of Western Europe and the United States in the creation of seminal ideas; nor is it to deny the construction of new "universalizing" models of modernity transcending narrow nationalism. What is at stake is the version of historical explanation. An obvious case is that of Frank Lloyd Wright, who never fitted into the overtidy explanations of the 1920s that the early historians (in Europe at least) wished to promote. Wright's works of the 1920s were considered too "romantic" or else too "personal" to concur with a "rationalist" ver-

5.1. Enrique del
Moral, Del Moral
House, view from
exterior court to
gallery, Tacubaya,
Mexico City, 1948.
Photo courtesy of
the Archive of
Louise Noelle
Merles.

sion of modernity and so were largely ignored, as if to say that they belonged to an earlier phase. Rudolph Schindler's remarkable early works in Southern California were consigned to a similar limbo. In fact, these artists were already opening the way to a profound reconsideration of the meaning of the American landscape, its ancient echoes, its varied climates, and its diverse technologies.[2] Through the local they aspired to their own version of universality.

There can be little doubt in retrospect that the early historians of Modern architecture felt a strong pressure to differentiate Modernism from any version of revivalism; in the 1930s the entire question of regional or national ingredients became taboo on account of Fascist and Nazi insistence upon traditionalist agendas. But in the process, a judicious analysis of the fusion of modern architectural concepts with local realities and myths was sacrificed. Le Corbusier's "primitivist" tendencies in the 1930s were never properly acknowledged or understood at the time, although they in fact revealed several ways of combining the natural and the mechanical, the international and the regional. When Sigfried Giedion came to formulate his epochal *Space, Time and Architecture* at the end of the 1930s, it was with the knowledge that the ideals he stood for were in danger in Europe, and with the intuition that the United States might supply a safe haven.[3] Giedion's Hegelian version of architectural development was attuned to the idea of a *zeitgeist,* or spirit of the times, and had no place for classical underpinnings or for regional inflections. The great emphasis accorded to Walter Gropius, and even to Gropius's first works in the United States, was hardly accidental, but it was a particular version of events. Curiously, and probably unconsciously, this version settled into place over a preexisting Yankee mythology that tended to assume that all that was best about North American culture arrived on the northeastern seaboard from Europe, then gradually spread its way from east to west across the continent.

If Wright after 1910 was one casualty of this approach, Latin American Modernism was another, and even today a balanced picture has not been fully achieved. It is salutary to recall that Luis Barragán's works at El Pedregal and at his own house at Tacubaya were realized at the same time as Gropius's Harkness Commons Dormitories at Harvard University—in the late 1940s.[4] But where the latter (in reality a work of decline) remained part of the transatlantic folklore of Modernism until recently, the former were scarcely acknowledged in the general literature of Modernism until the 1980s. Moreover, the integration of Latin American fragments into the dominant discourses has usually had recourse to an "exotic" terminology, as if the key artists were some sort of hothouse flowers.

The formulation of nationalist mythologies in Latin American contexts has scarcely helped matters, since these have tended to overstress the role of supposed local continuities and local "roots." It is, of course, an old story, this determination of North and South America to misunderstand one another. In the case of Mexico, the usual friction was perhaps exacerbated by entirely contrasting political schemes of modernization, and by a continuing amnesia north of the border about the degree of cultural continuity between the southwestern United States and Mexico. In any event, the emphasis upon a "Mexican" identity needs to be examined carefully for what it is: an ideological construct that has struggled with the problem of integrating new and old, Hispanic and pre-Hispanic, center and region, city and country, cosmopolitan and Indian, modern and mestizo, national and international. The much devalued word *regionalism* ("critical" or otherwise) has little place in this scenario, and even falls into the old trap of presuming a center and provinces in the global sphere.[5] Such a notion does not adequately describe the complexity of interchange that has formed part of the Mexican modern architectural development from its earliest days.

In fact, the very construct of "modernity" was an eclectic idea blending Enlightenment and earlier ideas, and the very concept of a "local tradition" had to engage with the sheer vastness and grandeur of a many-layered pre-Columbian heritage that could in no sense be confined to a "regional" pigeonhole. In the visual arts, at least, the role of a liberating abstraction was, in part, to escape the constriction of both imported European nineteenth-century models (e.g., those of the Belle Époque and of the Beaux Arts) and of a narrow neo-Colonial formulation, in favor of a far grander, "universalizing" vision that might encompass the vigor of Modernism and a mythologized version of the pre-Columbian traditions at the same time. This struggle to integrate diverse traditions, modern and ancient, runs through some of the architectural production in Mexico over the past sixty years and is unlikely to disappear simply on the basis of trade agreements.

These broad elements of the historical background are necessary in order to understand the Mexican architect Enrique del Moral, who was born in 1906 and who therefore was half a decade younger than Luis Barragán and half a decade older than Mario Pani. The latter was one of Del Moral's collaborators on the Ciudad Universitaria in Mexico City in the late 1940s and the early 1950s, and so it is easy to associate Del Moral's name with large-scale, "official" planning and with the transformation of the model of Le Corbusier's Ville Radieuse to deal with specifically Mexican institutional and topographic conditions. But Del Moral had a prodigious output as a designer at many scales, employing diverse technologies in countryside and in city. If his Mercado de la Merced of 1956 deserves to be considered in the context of inventive formal expression on the basis of a low-cost concrete and brick vaulting solution, his primary school in Casacuarán (1944–1946) takes its place in the history of modern buildings by making a frank acknowledgment of crude timber and brick construction and of rural vernacular traditions. It is evident in retrospect that even grand schemes such as that for the Ciudad Universitaria absorbed certain features of the wide spatial platforms of pre-Columbian tradition in their overall layout. Del Moral was an architect of wide learning and of broad historical vision who absorbed the doctrines of his teacher and first mentor José Villagrán García in the late 1920s, who adopted something of the "functionalist" doctrine as a purgative discipline, but who then went on to forge a personal position that integrated a certain ideal of spiritual and aesthetic enrichment into his program for a Modern architecture. Del Moral was aware at an early stage in his formation of Le Corbusier's writings and of the suggestion that architecture should transcend questions of construction in order to elevate the mind. He was also drawn to the poetic enrichment of the Modern plastic arts. By the end of the 1930s, Del Moral seems to have sensed that an attempt must be made to integrate ingredients of International Modern architecture with a judicious interpretation of specifically Mexican geographical and cultural conditions. He was not, of course, alone in this general quest (Barragán supplies an obvious parallel), but he still made a personal synthesis. Moreover, as suggested above, the late 1930s witnessed a new mood within Modernism, a subtle reaction against machinism in favor of "natural" values, as well as a plastic enrichment of the range of architectural devices for dealing with varying climates.[6]

The key to Del Moral's interpretation lay in his transformation of a basic type underlying many past eras of Mexican architecture and percussive in both the Hispanic and the pre-Hispanic periods, namely the *patio,* or the outdoor room. His reading of this basic type was not literal and was not attached to the architectural elements of any particular stylistic phase. In fact, Del Moral "reinvented" the patio around a largely personal mythology of the "Mexican personality," which he interpreted as being private, retiring, somewhat ambiguous, and grouped around the internal dynamics of the family and its quotidian patterns of behavior. Much of this emerged in the plan of his own house designed at Calle Francisco Ramírez 5 in Tacubaya in 1948. In a sense this house is a species of self-portrait as much as it is a particular interpretation of a cultural tendency, for it reflects only too clearly the artist's own retiring nature, as well as his discretion and elegance. The experience of moving through this building is an intense one, involving twists, turns, transitions, and strong contrasts of light and shade. The materials are textured and robust and include bold ochre walls, wide wooden plank floors with deep grooves, several lattices and grilles, rough masonry blocks, alabaster screens casting an amber glow, and deep black volcanic

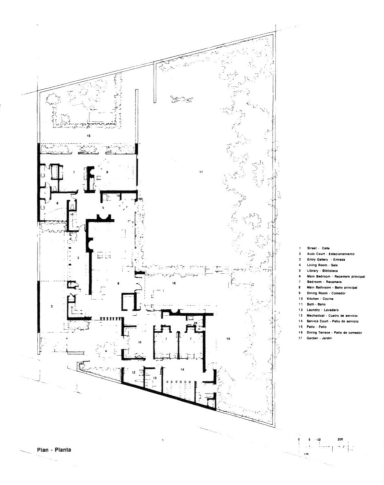

5.2. Enrique del Moral, Del Moral House, Ground Floor Plan, Tacubaya, Mexico City, 1948. Plan redrawn by Edward R. Burian.

1   Street · Calle
2   Auto Court · Estacionamiento
3   Entry Gallery · Entrada
4   Living Room · Sala
5   Library · Biblioteca
6   Main Bedroom · Recamara principal
7   Bedroom · Recamara
8   Main Bathroom · Baño principal
9   Dining Room · Comedor
10 Kitchen · Cocina
11 Bath · Baño
12 Laundry · Lavadero
13 Mechanical · Cuarto de servicio
14 Service Court · Patio de servicio
15 Patio · Patio
16 Dining Terrace · Patio de comedor
17 Garden · Jardin

Plan · Planta

5.3. Enrique del Moral, Del Moral House, view from garden court, Tacubaya, Mexico City, 1948. Photo courtesy of the Archive of Louise Noelle Merles.

5.4. Enrique del Moral, Del Moral House, interior view of living room, Tacubaya, Mexico City, 1948. Photo courtesy of the Archive of Louise Noelle Merles.

rock in some of the terrace floors. The visitor to the Del Moral House is guided quickly, but indirectly, to the most public spaces, the living room and the dining room, which are directly adjacent to the garden, the main unifying element of the entire arrangement. But there is always the sense of many other private lives beyond walls, screens, or partitions, and an inspection of the plan of the dwelling is enough to reveal subtle ways in which corridors and stairs are placed to ensure privacy and to demarcate the different "zones" of the building: the kitchen area adjacent to the small patio where one enters the complex; the master bedroom and its small secret garden and upstairs study to the rear of the site; and the guest apartment up some stairs immediately adjacent to the entrance.[7]

In fact this is no ordinary idea of a patio house at all, but rather resembles a species of labyrinth that is experienced as an unfolding set of layers, some of them tangible and visible, some of them invisible or implied. The experience involves separations, compressions, and expansions, and seems to reveal a deep fusion of certain features of Cubist space with other features that invoke, at a considerable geographical and historical distance, the spatial complexity of Arab architecture. It is not sufficiently acknowledged that the transplantation of Andalusian architecture to Latin America sometimes included this Arab residue, which then mingled with other ingredients on arrival.[8] The Barragán Residence of 1947, which stands just across the road from the Del Moral House, invokes these memories in a different form, one that is perhaps more directed toward a mystical silence, and one that contains a more overt Surrealism within its resonant abstraction. Here is not the place to develop an entire list of similarities and differences between Barragán and Del Moral, but it is as well to recognize a broader, embracing cultural agenda concerning the fusion of Modern architecture with several "substructures" and spatial ideas transformed from local and from other pasts.

It is at this point that one comes to the catalyst of modern transformation and to the central importance of Mies van der Rohe for both Del Moral and Barragán. The international influence of Mies has sometimes been discussed as if it were just a matter of steel and glass frames and of international big business. But there were many different aspects to Mies and to the way in which he was interpreted from afar, and in the case of the Del Moral House, it is the Mies of the Barcelona Pavilion, of the Tugendhat House, and of the several 1930s projects for patio

5.6. Enrique del Moral, Del Moral House, light quality at auto court, Tacubaya, Mexico City, 1948.

5.7. Enrique del Moral, Del Moral House, materials and tectonics of wall, Tacubaya, Mexico City, 1948. Photos by Edward R. Burian.

houses that is most telling. The spatial order of the Del Moral House relies upon all of these prototypes and transforms the planar wall of the original "international" models into something textured, almost rustic, and, as the architect himself would have it, "Mexican." But beyond the evident features of walls, glazed screens, platforms, steps, and overhanging roofs, there is also a concept of space—a concept that works with ambiguities of depth and that is attuned to the emotions and physical experience of the observer. Del Moral takes over this idea of modern space and injects it with a new density and texture, all the while bearing in mind Mies van der Rohe's overall intention: "to bring Nature, houses and people together into a higher unity."[9]

The Del Moral House was but one step in a long and complex career, but it succeeds in channeling and in condensing a multitude of intentions, some of them personal, others stemming from the energies and the dilemmas of a wider culture. This building and the architect who designed it deserve a wider audience than they have so far had, and I myself have now felt the need to integrate this particular work into the larger history of Modern architecture. Its immediate "neighbor" is the Barragán Residence across the road; but its "conceptual neighbors" are to be found far and wide in the transitional period of the late 1930s and the 1940s, when several other architects, in their respective societies, attempted their own fusions of what Del Moral called "the general and the local."[10]

Notes

1. In this regard, see Sigfried Giedion's *Space, Time and Architecture: The Growth of a New Tradition* and also Hitchcock and Johnson's *The International Style: Architecture Since 1922.*

2. Vincent Scully has discussed Wright in terms of his architecture's relationship to empathy, local culture, literature, and landscape in numerous books and articles, including *American Architecture and Urbanism.* I have also discussed this issue in my own book *Modern Architecture Since 1900.*

3. See Sigfried Giedion's *Space, Time and Architecture: The Growth of a New Tradition.*

4. See Emilio Ambasz's *The Architecture of Luis Barragán,* and my own essay "Laberintos intemporales" in *Arquitectura y Vivienda* (August 1988).

5. Although discussions of regionalism in American architecture date to the 1920s and beyond, the notion of critical regionalism came to the forefront in American schools of architecture in the 1980s. Among the major articles for this argument are two essays that appeared in *Center: A Journal for Architecture in America* 3, published in 1987 by University of Texas Press, Austin: Kenneth Frampton's "Ten Points on an Architecture of Regionalism: A Provisional Polemic," pp. 20-27; and Lawrence Speck's "Regionalism and Invention," pp. 8-19. For another point of view on this issue, see my own essay

"Towards an Authentic Regionalism" in *Mimar* 19 (Dec. 1985), which expands and develops ideas that I initially explored in *Modern Architecture Since 1900.*

6. Much of this information was garnered during my visit and conversation with Del Moral in January of 1985. See also Del Moral's essay "Tradición versus modernidad," S.E., Mexico City, 1954; Louise Noelle's "Semblanza del arquitecto Enrique del Moral" (1984) in *Enrique del Moral: Imagen y obra escogida* and *Arquitectos contemporáneos de México;* as well as Salvador Pinoncelly's *La obra de Enrique del Moral.*

7. See my essay "Arquitectura moderna, condiciones mexicanas" in L. Noelle, ed., *Teodoro González de León: La voluntad del creador,* pp. 29ff.

8. For a discussion on the influence of North African architecture on Luis Barragán, see Emilio Ambasz's *The Architecture of Luis Barragán,* pp. 105–108.

9. This quote by Mies is taken from Wolf Tegethoff's *Mies Van der Rohe: Villas and Country Houses,* p. 130.

10. These ideas are more fully developed in the third edition of my book *Modern Architecture Since 1900,* due to be released in 1996.

6   THE ARCHITECTURE OF JUAN O'GORMAN

Dichotomy and Drift

Edward R. Burian

We should not forget that men are only rational animals, and to proceed through any medium that is not the one of maximum efficiency through minimum effort, is not to proceed rationally.

—*Juan O'Gorman, from his 1933 address to the Mexican Congress of Architects*

We must remember the wonderful and fantastic architecture of Bomarzo near Viterbo, where the rooms of the guardians are heads of giants. The architect decided that the mouth be entry doors and the eyes windows. There you have an example of how fantasy, poetry, architecture and sculpture are integrated.

—*Juan O'Gorman, 1951*

Introduction

These statements by Juan O'Gorman (1905–1982), made nearly twenty years apart, set the stage for the discussion that follows. They reveal the range of concerns and architectural responses that mark O'Gorman's career and undoubtedly make him one of the most complex figures in the history of Modern architecture in post-Revolutionary Mexico. His prolific career is characterized by the crossing of boundaries between painting and architecture, political and aesthetic agendas, as well as several formal and technical languages. After even a cursory examination of O'Gorman's work, several obvious questions emerge: How can one make "sense" of this corpus of work? What are the issues that motivate the work? Why did he change?

While O'Gorman's paintings and murals have received considerable attention, his rich and complex architectural work and theoretical writings are often overlooked and merit broader critical attention. His work, like that of so many of his contemporaries in Mexico, is largely jettisoned by histories of Modern architecture. This may in part be due to the fact that his work is not a simple progression over a career and thus is not easily digested.

Previous commentators, such as C. B. Smith and Max Cetto, discuss O'Gorman's work primarily as a chronological listing of works. Ida Rodríguez Prampolini's excellent books primarily document his work in terms of a collection of interviews and essays written by O'Gorman and provide us with the most thorough record of his drawings. In context, what little has been written about O'Gorman typically characterizes his architectural work in terms of a cataclysmic shift from his earliest "functionalist" work to his "organic" work later in his career. Cetto states that O'Gorman's later work "is the pole opposite of classical objectivity, reason, fixed rules, faultless details (in which God is to be found according to Mies van der Rohe), for here the devil, contradiction and madness and dissolution reign supreme."[1] This view proposes the simple notion of progress across a career, of movement in one direction only, . . . of "this" to "that," of "rational" to "irrational," and also implies, although not directly stated, a moral dimension, that of the "fallen" modernist.

However, in more closely examining the work of O'Gorman four dichotomies emerge that can serve as a lens to bring his work into clearer focus.

The first of these dichotomies is the cosmopolitan and nativist, terms used by Octavio Paz in his discussions of Latin American poetry. This dichotomy is at the heart of O'Gorman's work as well as that of many of his contemporaries in Mexico. Artists in Mexico after the Revolution yearned to establish their Mexican identity through their work and also join the modern, Western tradition of the international avant-garde.[2]

The second dichotomy is the dilemma that Vincent Scully has termed the mechanic and the organic.[3] The mechanic embraces the image and processes of a rational, technologically driven machine age obsessed with progress, which utilizes abstraction as its mode of expression. The organic, on the other hand, embraces an architecture concerned with mythos, the land, and place.

The third dichotomy, between abstraction and figuration, follows from the second. Abstraction provides the means of expressing a universal architecture for a modern age. Figuration is initially an unintended but inevitable surplus meaning in O'Gorman's earliest "functionalist" work. Later in his career, the figurative and allegorical aspects of his architecture become more overt and direct.

The fourth dichotomy is between technology and representation. While these seem at first glance to be integrally related, they are, in fact, at odds with one another throughout most of O'Gorman's career. Initially, this dichotomy manifests itself in terms of machinelike imagery in the midst of the reality of

Mexican handcraft technology, and later in his career, in terms of the representation of a more mythic architecture of hand-made technology that accommodates the machines of the house.

An alternative way of understanding this complex architect is to view these dichotomies as woven into his entire architectural production as opposed to merely abandoning earlier agendas. O'Gorman's movement between dichotomies is bidirectional and omnidirectional rather than merely linear, and suggests an agenda that accommodates the complexity of modern life. Viewed in these terms, surplus meanings enrich his work. Furthermore, O'Gorman's own vacillation can be understood within the broader discussion of "drift" among an entire generation of Modern Mexican architects.

Background

A native of the Mexico City suburb of Coyoacán, O'Gorman was educated in Jesuit schools and initially studied medicine at the university. After being persuaded to study architecture, he graduated from the School of Architecture of the National University of Mexico in 1927. During the final two years of his education, he worked for three architects who were seminal modernists in Mexico: Carlos Obregón Santacilia, José Villagrán García, and Carlos Tarditi.[4] The influence of the theorist/practitioner Villagrán García was particularly important in that he was the leading advocate of Le Corbusier's theories in Mexico. In 1924, O'Gorman read Le Corbusier's *Towards a New Architecture* (by his own admission, four times) and selectively applied these theories in the design of twelve "functionalist" homes between 1928 and 1937. Like his mentor Villagrán García, O'Gorman initially embraced selective aspects of Le Corbusier's theories such as engineering, social programs, workers' housing, and the political nature of architecture.[5]

In the 1920s, Le Corbusier proposed a universal, antiregional architecture:

A house . . . will be a tool, just as the automobile is becoming a tool. The house will no longer be an ancient entity heavily rooted in the ground by deep foundations, an ancient symbol of the cult of the family and of the race.[6]

This prescription proved to be difficult to apply in the context of a culture such as Mexico's that was haunted by time and the agenda of racial affirmation posited by the post-Revolutionary regime.

In the thirties, O'Gorman was appointed chief architect of the Department of School Construction of the Ministry of Education, and he designed and built thirty primary schools, as well as a technical school in Mexico City. Reverting back to his initial medical education, O'Gorman compared schools to hospitals in terms of their need for cleansing:

In schools are we going to think of the spiritual necessities? In the face of a character problem of such transcendency and responsibility, are we going to dwell on artistic terms or enjoyable aspects or on the spiritual aspects of the building, when what we need is hygiene? Hygiene of the body and intelligence. . . . If we establish this matter under the real basis of inexpensive schools, economically built, with durable materials, and as efficient as possible in spending the pueblo's money, the Mexican pueblo, we would see that what is mistakenly called Nordic architecture is in reality only the applied knowledge of construction and composition. . . . Architecture will have to become more international because of the simple reason that, daily, men become more universal. Is this not the role of education? Is it not the role of industry? Thanks to these factors, in Mexico we may have the comfort and well-being that technology provides.[7]

He continued his involvement with education in the thirties by founding the School of Engineering and Architecture (Escuela de Ingeniería y Arquitectura [ESIA]) of the National Polytechnic Institute with Juan Legarreta. The founding of the school made explicit O'Gorman's commitment, at this point in his career, to an architecture that was primarily concerned with technical and rational systems.

In the 1930s, O'Gorman viewed architecture as a functional and instrumental response to human needs. He believed, at this time, that human needs could be rationally understood and precisely enumerated, logically resulting in appropriate solutions that could be universally applied. Ironically, this view echoed the discredited *científicos* (scientists) of the recently overthrown Porfirio Díaz administration who advocated a specifically Comtian version of Positivism in Mexico in which society (and architecture) was conceived as a mathematical construct and was progress oriented.[8] In his address to the Conference of the Society of Mexican Architects in 1933, O'Gorman makes this emphatic when he states:

On the other hand, the essential needs for all men are known values, exact and precise. The size of the door to a laborer's house will be the same as the door to the philosopher's house. . . . Man invented architecture not to copy something that harmed him, something that punished and offended him, but to liberate himself from that certain aspect that was his enemy, *nature!* Life imposes its economical, social, and material conditions. Technique is the means to resolve this in a better way. (By means of the better path, the maximum efficiency for the minimum effort.) This is to proceed rationally. Fellow architects: I believe that the architecture that solves the material, palpable needs that are not mistaken, that truly exist and at the same time that are fundamental and general to humans, is the real and unique architecture of our epoch.[9]

6.1. Juan O'Gorman, Preliminary Scheme for Federal District Workers Housing, Mexico City, early 1930s. Photo courtesy of the Archive of Louise Noelle Merles.

Belying his pluralistic agenda, O'Gorman expressed difficulty in reconciling "the sentimental factors, the human needs" in relation to his agenda of technological rationalism. O'Gorman stated that "it is undeniable that all men have feelings that are the product of life and experience; however, are we going to allow these to have a harmful, prejudicial influence in the solution of architectural problems, as these feelings or spiritual reasons are only needed by those that possess them?"[10] It was the struggle of this ambiguous dilemma, along with the desire to create a national "Mexican" architecture, that would characterize his career and that would ultimately lead to the transformation of his architectural *oeuvre*.

The Ambiguity of Functionalism

Several authors have questioned the relationship of Functionalism to Modern architecture. Stanford Anderson has claimed that "functionalism has dulled our understanding of the theories and practice of modern architecture." He goes on to state that "no description of function, however thorough, will automatically translate into architectural form . . . not even self-proclaimed functionalists could fulfill their program without recourse to other form generators."[11]

In *Theory and Design in the First Machine Age*, Reyner Banham proposed that Functionalism may have had an "austere nobility, but it was poverty-stricken symbolically."

The architecture of the Twenties, though capable of its own austerity and nobility, was heavily loaded with symbolic meanings that were discarded or ignored by its apologists of the Thirties. . . . Emotion had played a much larger part than logic in the creation of the style . . . it was no more inherently economical style than any other. The true aim of the style had clearly been, to quote Gropius' words about the Bauhaus and its relation to the world of the Machine Age, . . . "to invent and create forms symbolizing the world, and it is in respect to such symbolic forms that its historical justification must lie."[12]

O'Gorman's difficult reconciliation between what he called "technological conditions" and "aesthetic conditions" was revealed in a diagram from the 1930s. In it he showed that technical and aesthetic considerations were almost equal, with a slight weighting toward technical criteria. He attempted to analyze design as a rational, scientific, and mathematical process that acknowledged the equivocation of aesthetic impulses. At this point in his career, O'Gorman felt the need to control the design process in an attempt to secure its legitimacy. In this way, the emotional was licensed by the rational.

The "Functionalist" Architecture of O'Gorman in the 1930s

The examination of specific works of architecture by O'Gorman demonstrates the dichotomous nature of his *oeuvre*. While the projects range in scale and program from residences and gardens to institutional projects, each is an attempt to resolve seemingly opposed issues.

O'Gorman's architecture was initially conceived in the aftermath of the Mexican Revolution in which the post-Revolutionary government had a political agenda for art, most clearly illustrated by the Mexican Mural movement. O'Gorman wished to embrace the idea of Functionalism, selectively extricated from

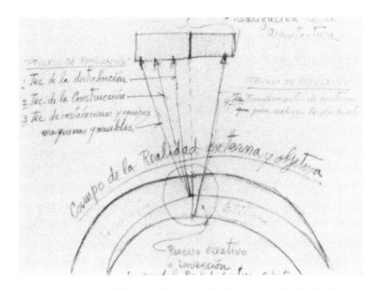

6.2. Diagram by Juan O'Gorman demonstrating the process of design in relation to the technical process of realization and the balance between technical and aesthetic considerations. Courtesy of Ida Rodríguez Prampolini, previously published in Ida Rodríguez Prampolini, Juan O'Gorman, arquitecto y pintor.

the writings of Le Corbusier, and yet felt politically and emotionally connected to the ideas espoused in the notion of *mexicanidad,* that is, a concern for local culture and uniquely Mexican themes. This concern mirrors the great struggle of modern Mexican art and Mexican culture in general, that of wanting to participate in the European avant-garde as a member of the modern intellectual community (particularly French), and yet engage more Mexican themes concerned with the specifics and culture of place. For O'Gorman, this juggling act was not one of total exclusion of one idea in favor of the other, but rather of the weighting and prioritizing of both notions that are threaded throughout his architectural career. Later in his career, technical rationalism was not completely rejected, but rather subsumed into an exploration of Surrealism and organic architecture.

In 1933, as part of a series of "functionalist" houses designed by him, O'Gorman completed a house for Dr. Luis Erro that had an attached astronomical observatory. The latter feature makes a structurally redundant, anthropomorphic gesture and is oddly "rooted" to the ground by a member that appears to penetrate the observatory raised on pilotis. This mysterious component is

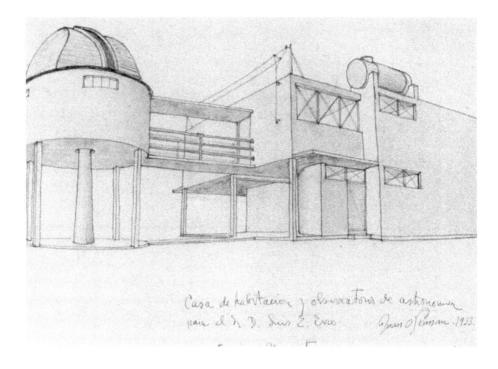

Casa de habitación y observatoria de astronomia
para el S. D. Luis E Erro   Juan O'Gorman 1933.

6.3. Juan O'Gorman, Residence and Observatory for Dr. Luis Erro, Tlaco-quemécatl, Mexico City, 1933. Courtesy of Ida Rodríguez Prampolini, previously published in Ida Rodríguez Prampolini, Juan O'Gorman, arquitecto y pintor.

devoted to nocturnal functions and the observation of the heavens, which were traditionally the domain of female divinities in many ancient cultures, including pre-Columbian culture.[13] This function is so mysterious that it is held at a distance from the main body of the building, as if it might contaminate the rest. The massing of this figure suggests a helmeted pre-Columbian figure, recalling monumental Olmec sculpture. Like many of his houses at the time, the "guts" of the house, including the utility connections and water tank, are exposed on the outside.

The following year O'Gorman designed a studio and apartment for the noted American anthropologist and editor of a guide to Mexico Frances Toor. Unlike the earlier houses, the project became more nativist and "Mexicanized." Vernacular urban design strategies, programmatic functions, colors, and interior furnishings were used as expressive devices. Outdoor washing and laundry areas appeared on the ground floor, and the rooftop followed the prescriptions of Le Corbusier as well as traditional Mexican typologies of inhabiting the roof in warm summer months. The building respected the traditional urban fabric by

6.4. Juan O'Gorman, street facade, Studio and Apartment for Frances Toor, Calle Hamburgo, Mexico City, 1934. Photo courtesy of the Archive of Louise Noelle Merles.

establishing a wall at the street that was a gateway for cars and a planted wall that prefigured its use in the Kahlo/Rivera studio. The colors of vernacular Mexican architecture also made their appearance. The exterior walls were painted deep blue, and the figural stair at ground level is venetian red. While the vivid coloration of the walls recalled Le Corbusier's earlier work at Pessac and La Roche, the house reflected the culture of specific Mexican types.

The interior of the studio was filled with Toor's collections of folk art. The juxtaposition of abstract, gridded, universalized structural slab and industrialized steel windows with anthropomorphic folk art was surreal and was an essential way to Mexicanize the house. Folk art was used by politically motivated artists and intellectuals in Mexico in the thirties as a way of identifying with indigenous Mexican themes and was sanctioned by the Mexican government.

6.5. Juan O'Gorman, Kahlo/Rivera Studios, view from street with Rivera's studio on the left and Kahlo's studio to the right, San Angel, Mexico City, 1930. Photo courtesy of the Archive of Louise Noelle Merles.

In addition, several unintended anthropomorphic gestures occurred in the composition and experience of the project. The massing of the building, with its twin gates, and the building's plan can be read as a mask or seated figure, prefiguring O'Gorman's later work, while the stair that pins through the building recalls a spine.

The Kahlo/Rivera Studios

The Kahlo/Rivera studios have received renewed attention since the "canonization" of Frida Kahlo in the United States during the 1980s. In 1929, after O'Gorman built his own studio in San Angel to demonstrate his theories of Functionalism, Diego Rivera bought a portion of the property and built a studio and house for Frida, which were completed in 1931. The siting of the residence was explicit in its rejection of the modernist conception of the residence as a freestanding object in terms of a site and urban design strategy. In the Kahlo/Rivera studios, as well as in a house for Julio Castellanos and other works, a landscaped wall of cordon cactus at the edge of the site was used to establish outdoor rooms in the traditional Mexican manner, and it prefigures the use of vegetal-dominant imagery in his Surrealist paintings of the forties. In addition, this project was the most spatially complex of all of O'Gorman's functionalist work in terms of its siting and the manipulation of the building section.

The exterior colors were "Indian" red and deep blue, while the interior colors were yellow and parrot green. The deep blue color was similar to that Kahlo used in her own house in Coyoacán, *azul añil*, "a deep matte blue color traditionally used in Mexican houses to ward off evil spirits."[14] The "Indian" red wall color recalled the *tezontle*, or volcanic stone, traditional to Mexico City since the pre-Columbian and colonial eras, and has, as Octavio Paz has commented, the color of dried blood. The terrazzo floor in the Rivera studio was a riot of color made with colored stone chips and was expressed as a distinct element from the walls. All steel fenestration and steel metalwork were painted orange vermilion. The traditional vernacular colors utilized in the exterior facades of the Kahlo/Rivera studios related the architecture to the culture of the place. This reflected O'Gorman's interest in making an architecture concerned with progress, universality, technological rationalism, and abstraction and yet that also utilized vernacular Mexican colors and indigenous art to create interiors.

The studios were tectonically conceived as a rational system of concrete frame and waffle slab, where walls are infilled between

137

6.6. Juan O'Gorman, Rivera Studio, San Angel, Mexico City, 1930. Photo courtesy of the Archive of Louise Noelle Merles.

the frame, unlike the contrasting discrete enclosure systems of Le Corbusier's work of the period. Glazing consisted of steel industrialized windows that formed a fine overall pattern and, in some respects, prefigured O'Gorman's later use of patterned mosaics in his architecture.

The interiors were quite distinct from Le Corbusier's work of the time. In houses such as the Villa Savoye, interior surfaces were smooth and uninterrupted, with concealed wiring and plumbing. Photographs of Le Corbusier's interiors show that he used industrial objects, Cubist paintings, views to landscapes, and objects of a healthy life to project an image of modernity, physical well-being, and a controlled sense of order.

In the Kahlo/Rivera residence the interiors were expressed as distinct, separate elements. Mechanical and electrical systems were exposed in the studios. All pipes were visible, and electrical power runs and connections were used as expressive compositional elements reminiscent of veins and arteries. The machines of the house, such as the shower, were proudly presented as aids to health and cleansing. Ironically, although machine technology was utilized as an expressive device, the building was produced by inexpensive hand labor. Thus, the technology of the building simulated the image of machine mass-production techniques of a modern, industrialized world. This dichotomy presented itself throughout the history of Modern architecture in Mexico, in the sense that the representation of industrialized systems of construction did not correspond to the realities of handcraft technology.

The interiors of Kahlo's and Rivera's studios were striking and surreal and prefigured O'Gorman's later architecture. Both Rivera and Kahlo were avid collectors of indigenous art. Huge "Judas" figures hung inside,[15] which served to create a surreal sense of dislocation and the fantastic, and to locate this universalized conception of architecture unmistakably in Mexico.

As Beatriz Colomina has pointed out, in the work of Le Corbusier, the window wall acted as a camera lens for capturing and categorizing the landscape.[16] Like the work of Le Corbusier, the Rivera studio acted as a hooded camera lens and framing device for capturing and categorizing views of the landscape, while its cantilevered window wall gestured toward the city. However, this glazing system also had the possibility for curtains to be closed across the lower portion of the window wall, thus creating an interior framing device for occupants and fantastic indigenous art.

In Rivera's painting *The Painter's Studio* (1954), a reclining woman turns provocatively toward the viewer with eyes cast upward toward the seemingly limitless extension of the gridded ceiling. She is dominated on all sides by skeletons and half-human, half-animal figures, pre-Columbian art, and an animal-like machine. The grid of the ceiling plane serves as a frame and device for focusing and contrasting the objects, inhabitants, and visitors to the studio. Significantly, it is also used as a contrasting device within the frames of Rivera's paintings. The curtain is closed across the lower portion of the window wall, and the exterior landscape visible through the upper portion of the window wall is indicated as a blurred schematic. Both human and inanimate objects are selectively placed in focus as though by a camera lens.

O'Gorman's

Painting in

Relationship to

the Development

of Architectural

Themes

After experiencing dissatisfaction with architectural practice, O'Gorman devoted himself to easel and mural painting from approximately 1936 to 1948. O'Gorman believed that functionalist architecture in Mexico had become corrupted by developers who wanted to build the least for the maximum profit. He claimed that the result of this was the creation of an architecture of negligible qualities for the user and for Mexico. He also felt that architects who practiced in the mode of this reductivist architecture cladded their buildings in inappropriate and expensive materials. "In 1938, as I did not know where to turn from functionalism, and I had no intention of becoming a businessman, I abandoned architecture as a profession, and became a painter."[17] At this point in his career, O'Gorman developed in his painting the themes of *mexicanidad* and industrial production that had earlier been explored in his architecture.

In O'Gorman's painting *The City of Mexico* (1949), hands extend from beyond the frame, drawing the viewer inside. The mestizo construction worker is portrayed as an ennobled, yet anonymous and universal, component of the technical production of architecture, while a variety of devices in the painting allude to pre-Columbian and colonial culture. In his painting *The Myths* (1942), O'Gorman's interest in the integration of the organic and mechanic becomes explicit. Surrealism seemed a way of accessing a lost pre-Columbian grandeur buried in the subconscious of Mexico. In a fantastic world reminiscent of Hieronymus Bosch, buildings literally grow out of the earth. Human, divine, and animal figures inhabit a world where heaven, reality, and underworld are intertwined. Ancient myths are integrated with the technology of the present, and the body becomes both animal and vegetal. Anonymous workers, who appear in the upper right-hand corner with their backs to the viewer, call our attention to the means of production and provide a jarring confrontation with the reality presented in the painting.

In 1951 O'Gorman collaborated with Gustavo Saavedra and Juan Martínez de Velasco on the main library at the University City. His original scheme was to propose a pre-Columbian type, a mythic pyramid, to house the main library at the center of the campus. This proposal implied that the library was to be the most important building on the campus, that pre-Columbian culture was intended to be idealized, and that the acquisition of knowledge was a sacred act. However, this proposal was rejected as

6.7. Juan O'Gorman, The City of Mexico, 1949. Courtesy of Museo de Arte Moderno, Mexico City.

unacceptable to the campus architects because of the abstract, "International Style" vocabulary of the rest of the new campus.[18] The scheme was modified to a practically windowless stack tower, sitting on a base of support functions. The building had few figural and sculptural gestures in its massing, and the allegorical layering of the facade was reduced to a wall plane in which the building itself became a canvas for representation. O'Gorman used this canvas to create a mural that represented a shift to a didactic, symbolic, allegorical architecture, utilizing the mythological imagery, and occasionally the compositional devices, from pre-Columbian culture. In one of the landmark symbols of Modern Mexican architecture, O'Gorman was able to reconnect to a mythical past for political and racial purposes. The scale of the facade and its position near the center of the campus implied that it performed a public, ritualistic function of both witnessing and suggesting collective activities of the student body.

This mural mosaic technique, which utilized native materials and handcraft technology, was also realized at Diego Rivera's residence/museum/tomb, Anhuacalli (1944), and his Lerma Waterworks Project (1951) in Mexico City, as well as in O'Gorman's own mural project at Taxco. However, at the main library a hybrid handcraft/industrialized technology was utilized. The native stone was set by hand in a predetermined pattern in a

6.8. Juan O'Gorman, Gustavo M. Saavedra, and Juan Martínez de Velasco; Central Library, Ciudad Universitaria (University City), Mexico City, 1950–1952. Photo by Edward R. Burian.

modular concrete panel, which was hoisted into place by machines.

Masks and anthropomorphic relationships exist at a variety of scales in the composition of the mosaic facades of the library, including a "Tlaloc-like," goggle-eyed figure, with a short, centralized strip of corridor for a nose facing west, another figure at the penthouse, and numerous superimposed masks and figures at a smaller scale, which form an overall pattern telling the story of Mexican and human history.

The Pedregal

House and the

Utilization of

Pre-Columbian

Themes and

Imagery

In the 1950s, O'Gorman built his own extraordinary, idiosyncratic residence among the lava beds of Pedregal in Mexico City. Its style recalled the "grotesque" architecture and gardens of the Italian Renaissance as well as the pre-Columbian use of monumental masks, particularly in Mayan architecture.[19] In contrast to the library tower at the university, O'Gorman here utilized a sculptural and plastic formal vocabulary that was fully integrated with the topography of the site.

Pre-Columbian imagery was romanticized and utilized in this period of O'Gorman's architecture. Masklike figures refer to Tlaloc (god of rain), with his characteristic earplugs, as well as to numerous other figures of pre-Columbian iconography. The walls were crafted of hand-laid stone covered by stone mosaic. The materials of the stone mosaic were composed of twelve colors of sedimental and volcanic rock indigenous to Mexico (only the blue mosaic stone was not a natural mineral).[20]

The siting of the residence was particularly meaningful in that the eye-shaped window in the tower faced east toward Popocatepetl and Ixtaccihuatl, sacred mountains in the pre-Columbian culture.

The plan organization, while merging with the site at the perimeter, still utilized principles of composition from his earlier, functionalist work. The cores were rationally conceived and stacked back to back, while the gridded industrialized glazing systems were juxtaposed with the wall/cave enclosure system.

Conclusions:

O'Gorman,

Organic

Architecture,

and Drift

O'Gorman's shift in agenda stems in part from his reevaluation of Corbusian Functionalism in relation to Wrightian organic architecture.

I realized long ago that it was unfortunate that Le Corbusier and not Frank Lloyd Wright caught our attention. Wright would have helped us stay closer to our true American tradition. . . . Taliesin [West], the greatest modern project built in this century, . . . has a recognizable Mexican character. It revives Meso-American tradition. It was Wright . . . who understood organic architecture as related to the human being in his geographical and historical content."[21]

O'Gorman further refines his definition of organic architecture when he states that it entails "a relation directly with the geography and history of the place . . . a harmonic relationship of man

6.9. Juan O'Gorman, O'Gorman Residence, exterior, El Pedregal, Mexico City, 1951. Photo courtesy of the Archive of Louise Noelle Merles.

and earth."[22] O'Gorman's interest in the work of Frank Lloyd Wright is particularly significant in the sense that Wright was also interested in many of the same dichotomies, in particular, as Vincent Scully has pointed out, the synthesis of the organic and the mechanic. In an introduction to a book on traditional Mexican homes written in 1980, O'Gorman makes this break with mainstream Modernism even more explicit:

It now seems clear that the International Style of modern architecture applied to residential buildings has worn out . . . most people are fed up with the mechanical so-called style of the Bauhaus. . . . All the folk architecture that has been inherited from the past is an excellent source of inspiration to be applied and used to great advantage in modern houses because it has the necessary elements that are in accordance with the function and the climate

6.10. Juan O'Gorman, O'Gorman Residence, interior, El Pedregal, Mexico City, 1951. Photo courtesy of the Archive of Louise Noelle Merles.

of the region in which they were done . . . regional methods of construction also achieve natural simplicity which is not only more pleasant to live with, but also cheaper to make.[23]

It is interesting to note that even at this point in his career, O'Gorman still justifies his interest in vernacular Mexican architecture in functional and rational terms.

The shift in O'Gorman's work can be thought of in terms of the larger issue of "drift" among Mexican modernists. Several leading Mexican modernists, such as Díaz Morales and the Guadalajara School, and even Barragán and Legorreta (who at one time was a partner of Villagrán García's), vacillate between modernist abstraction and traditional figuration during their careers. This can be attributed to a number of factors: the strong-rooted traditions of vernacular architecture, tectonic considerations, and the realities of handcraft technology in Mexico, as well as the influence and interest in vernacular Mexican themes by artists such as Rufino Tamayo, María Izquierdo, and others.

In *The Shape of Time,* George Kubler discusses the necessity of humans to recall ancient mythic cultures:

The retention of old things has always been a central ritual in human societies. . . . In a wider perspective the ancestor cults of primitive tribes have a similar purpose, to keep present some record of the power and knowledge of vanished peoples.[24]

The representation of ancient ancestor cultures for O'Gorman provides a way of laying claim to the power of a virtually vanished culture and religion that are "safe" because they belong to a mythic past.[25]

O'Gorman used construction technology as a way to express specific ideologies at various points in his architectural career, whether used as a representation of progress and rationalism or ultimately as a reconnection to the mythic pre-Columbian past, nature, and the earth. O'Gorman initially conceived of technology as being at the service of humanity, for its comfort and well-being; later in his career, as a way of demonstrating the resistance of the handmade in a technological, modern world; and ultimately, as a way to dwell inside the earth and be integrated with nature.

The wrestling with these dichotomies reflects the complexity of modern life in post-Revolutionary Mexico. This acceptance of diverse influences in fact characterizes much of the production of

Mexican art and architecture after the pre-Columbian era (and even during the pre-Columbian era in some respects), especially with regard to the intermingling of races and culture, or the *mestizaje* aspects of colonial culture in Mexico.

The work of O'Gorman expresses a variety of anthropomorphic relationships. The early functionalist work is hygienic in that it utilizes a biological metaphor by means of the articulation of systems, and anthropocentric in that this process of ordering space produced a hygienic, human domination over nature.[26] In his later organic work, the anthropomorphic metaphor is more literal and direct. Masks from a mythic past and the human body are used as a direct system of representation. In his own house, architecture, earth, and garden merge.

His work represents an immense struggle to produce an authentic Mexican architecture. Over the course of his career it reflects the tension between seemingly opposed dichotomies: the cosmopolitan and the nativist, the mechanic and the organic, abstraction and figuration, technology and representation, and ironically, his privileged upbringing and his own Trotskyite views. O'Gorman embraces the pre-Columbian past in an attempt to reclaim an embedded lost consciousness; the pre-Columbian past is a national resource of potential meaning to be unlocked in the psyche of the people. It is analogous in many respects to the ideas that were being explored by the Surrealist artists of the time. While O'Gorman's exact relationship with Surrealism, as an international movement and in its particular manifestation in Mexico, is unclear, it is a subject for further study that may shed much light on his motivations and conceptual agenda.

Ultimately, O'Gorman's work forms a critical point of departure in the development of Modern architecture in Mexico in that he produced an extraordinary body of varied work. In this way, he opened the door for many architects in Mexico that would follow him, in that he questioned the nature of orthodox Modernism in Mexico.

Notes

1. See the passionate introductory essay by Max Cetto in *Modern Architecture in Mexico*, p. 28. Cetto presents an argument for Modern Mexican architecture as a response to "national traits" and as an extension of pre-Columbian tradition, typical of many commentators of the time.

2. See the essay "Mexican Art of the Twentieth Century," by Dore Ashton, in *Mexico Splendors of Thirty Centuries*, p. 558.

3. For a further discussion of this issue, see the article by Vincent Scully entitled

"Architecture: The Natural and the Manmade" in *Denatured Visions: Landscape and Culture in the Twentieth Century,* pp. 7–19.

4. C. B. Smith, *Builders in the Sun: Five Mexican Architects,* p. 18.

5. Ibid.

6. See M. Piacentini, "Le Corbusier's 'The Engineers Aesthetic: Mass Production Houses,'" originally published in *Architettura e Arti Decorative II* (1922), pp. 220–223.

7. See Juan O'Gorman's address, "Arquitectura contemporánea," presented at the Conferencia en la Sociedad de Arquitectos, Mexico City, 1933, published in Ida Rodríguez Prampolini's *Juan O'Gorman: Arquitecto y pintor,* pp. 69–77. In further conversations with Antonio Toca in the summer of 1995, Toca mentioned that in 1975, O'Gorman gave a lecture at the UAM in which he emphasized the necessity of hygiene in his specifications for his proposals for workers' housing, because he believed that they were usually very "unkempt."

8. For an elaboration of this discussion of the role Comte's philosophy played in the Díaz regime, see P. Romanell's *The Making of the Mexican Mind,* pp. 42–66.

9. Juan O'Gorman's address, "Arquitectura contemporánea," pp. 69–77.

10. Ibid.

11. See S. Anderson's essay "The Fiction of Function," in a collection of papers from a conference entitled *Putting Modernity in Its Place.*

12. See R. Banham's *Theory and Design in the First Machine Age,* pp. 320–330.

13. For example, see M. E. Miller's *The Art of Mesoamerica from Olmec to Aztec,* p. 72, for a discussion of female divinities in the courtyard of the Pyramid of the Moon at Teotihuacán, among numerous other examples of female nocturnal goddesses in Mesoamerican culture.

14. T. Street-Porter, *Casa Mexicana,* p. 155.

15. Ibid. These figures were traditionally filled with firecrackers and exploded on the feast of Sábado de Gloria (the Saturday before Easter) and symbolize the betrayal of Judas and the people by their oppressors.

16. For a discussion of Le Corbusier's architecture as a viewing mechanism, see Beatriz Colomina's essay "The Split Wall: Domestic Voyeurism" in *Sexuality & Space.* For a broader discussion of the idea of the body and sexuality, see the articles by Beatriz Colomina published in *Assemblage* (December 1992) and *AA Files* 20 (Autumn 1990). For a discussion on the importance of the body in relationship to the conception, making, and experience in architecture, see Alberto Pérez-Gómez's article "The Renovation of the Body: John Hejduk and the Cultural Relevance of Theoretical Projects" in *AA Files* 13, among his other writings on the subject.

17. C. B. Smith, *Builders in the Sun: Five Mexican Architects,* p. 18.

18. Ibid.

19. For examples of pre-Columbian masks at an architectural scale, see the following sites: La Venta (Olmec culture); Temple of Quetzalcóatl and Tlaloc masks (Teotihuacán culture); Cerros, Uaxactún, Tikal, Palenque, Yaxchilán, Copán, Uxmal (Maya culture); among others. For a more complete discussion, see Mary Ellen Miller's *The Art of Mesoamerica from Olmec to Aztec* and Doris Heyden and Paul Gendrop's *Pre-Columbian Architecture of Mesoamerica.*

20. Esther McCoy (Obituary), *Progressive Architecture* (March 1982), p. 27.

21. C. B. Smith, *Builders in the Sun: Five Mexican Architects,* p. viii.

22. Ibid.

23. Juan O'Gorman, Introduction to *Tradition of Craftsmanship in Mexican Homes,* p. viii. The text to this book was written by Patricia W. O'Gorman, niece of Juan O'Gorman.

24. G. Kubler, *The Shape of Time: Remarks on the History of Things,* p. 82.

25. For an elaboration of this issue, see my interview with Alberto Pérez-Gómez in this book.

26. These insights and several others in this paper were offered by Steven Moore, who generously commented on many aspects of this essay.

THE ARCHITECTURE

OF CARLOS OBREGÓN SANTACILIA

A Work for Its Time and Context

Carlos G. Mijares Bracho

Translated by Edward R. Burian and Antonio E. Méndez-Vigatá

It is clear that individual works of architecture form a critical component of the urban context and shape the form of the city. It is also important to note that the presence, experience, and, on occasion, the memory of buildings and places are among the many possible readings of architecture.

These readings are the focus of this essay, the readings of an architect's work through the experiences of another architect. The works include those that have contributed to the urban order of the city, which were created when I was beginning my professional education, and others that have since ceased to exist. My intent in this essay is to reintroduce Carlos Obregón Santacilia's work to an audience that barely knows of its existence, and also to provide a brief and necessary personal homage.

I am speaking about this work from the perspective of an architect who repeatedly experiences and passes by Obregón's buildings, who enters, departs, and at times lingers inside them. Unfortunately, because many of his works have been eradicated from the face of the city, the memory of these buildings is sometimes all that remains.

Some architects' works are important for the moment and also transcend their specific epoch, yet are infrequently investigated, analyzed, or evaluated. The work of Carlos Obregón Santacilia (1896–1961) is an example of this phenomenon. Perhaps his obscurity lies in the fact that he followed a path that was not commonly accepted and he was inclined to simultaneously maintain certain traditional values as well as the dictates of the vanguard. He also instigated and endured disagreements with his colleagues who controlled the limited architectural media of the time in Mexico. Because his was an architecture of transition that was difficult to categorize in terms of a specific style and consistency, his work has not received its due attention.

7.1. Carlos Obregón Santacilia, Secretaría de Salubridad y Asistencia (Ministry of Health and Assistance), exterior view, Mexico City, 1925. Photo courtesy of INBA, Dirección de Arquitectura.

Born into a well-to-do family, the seventh of ten brothers, Carlos Obregón Santacilia was the maternal great-grandson of one of Mexico's greatest presidents, Benito Juárez. His father was a physician, and his mother nurtured in her son a profound social consciousness and artistic sensibility. Early in his life, the family was based in Guanajuato, a city with a rich fabric of colonial architecture. Prior to the Mexican Revolution, he also spent considerable time at the family's hacienda in the countryside outside the city. In this cultural mix, Obregón Santacilia developed conciliatory political views with a liberal attitude toward social issues inherited from the legacy of Benito Juárez, yet with a tolerant, moderate attitude toward the church. Although conservative friends of the family were reluctant for him to attend the Academy of San Carlos, he received his Beaux Arts education from this institution, where he developed extraordinary drawing skills and was exposed to the writings of Julien Guadet and Louis Cloquet, among others. Soon after graduation he began to practice professionally and was able to secure a number of government-sponsored commissions.

7.2. Carlos Obregón Santacilia, Secretaría de Salubridad y Asistencia (Ministry of Health and Assistance), detail, Mexico City, 1925. Photo by Edward R. Burian.

A brief examination of his architecture reveals the idiosyncratic

nature of his work. One aspect of this is his capacity to express, generally with a great deal of skill, many diverse modes of composition.

Between 1922 and 1925, coinciding with the beginning of his professional practice, he designed the Mexico Pavilion for the Rio de Janeiro Exposition (1922)[1] in a "delirious" neo-Colonial Baroque style. The same year, also in Rio de Janeiro, in the Monument for Cuauhtémoc designed in collaboration with the architect Carlos Tarditi, he explored a nationalistic *aztequizante* (Aztec National) style. In 1923 he remodeled the Ministry of Foreign Relations Building in a "French" style, which Obregón good-humoredly referred to as "some vague Louis the . . .?" His professional thesis in 1924 for the Benito Juárez School, which was actually built about that time, has a colonial vocabulary that was much more restrained than that of the Mexico Pavilion and responded directly to the nationalistic concerns expressed and promoted by José Vasconcelos in terms of his diverse ambitions for culture. The project for the School of the Blind, Deaf, and Mute (1924–1925) had a volumetric development and treatment very unencumbered with stylistic references to the past and was clearly intended to be an abstract, functional building.

The Santacilia Building (1925–1929) began to demonstrate some characteristics of a formal language that was to become his own. The remodeling of the interiors of the Bank of Mexico (1926–1928) overtly utilized Art Deco composition, which he had only used schematically in other projects, such as the building for the Department of the Federal District (1926), realized in collaboration with José Villagrán García, an architect who rapidly became the leading academic proponent of modern theory in Mexico at the time. Obregón continued to utilize the Art Deco mode of composition more or less consistently for both private houses and subsequent major buildings.

In these same years (1925–1929), in the splendid building for the Ministry of Health, he created a work that was a successful synthesis of his influences and antecedents that could be described as *obregonista,* a term that is singularly descriptive in that it evokes both the architect and the recent president of the republic, General Alvaro Obregón (1920–1924), who gave active support to the cultural movement of the time.

Around the 1930s, the architect realized a large number of projects for private residences that continued to show the variety of influences and styles that characterized his work, from the magnificent residence for Manuel Gómez Morín (1931) in a surprising contemporary language (a language that in later years culminated in his own vacation home in Acapulco) to the Neoclassic design for Federico Lachica (1930) or his own residence in Tlacopac (1930–1931) with reminiscences of colonial architecture. This attitude persisted in the area of residential projects with the residence for Alberto J. Pani (1934), in a fortunate blend of nationalistic Art Deco, and in another abstracted neo-Colonial residence for Señora Pani de Covarrubias.

The 1938 projects for the Cine Coliseo [Coliseum Theater] and for the offices of the Seguros de Mexico [Insurance of Mexico] presented a slightly eccentric, but interesting, abstract, functionalist architecture. At this stage of his career, the diversity of projects and proposals, including those related to mass housing as well as urban proposals, reflected the breadth of his interests and professional skills.

Without a doubt, the decade of the thirties consolidated the expression and richness of Obregón's architectural vocabulary in projects that were more personal and significant: the Monument

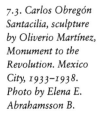

7.3. Carlos Obregón Santacilia, sculpture by Oliverio Martínez, Monument to the Revolution. Mexico City, 1933–1938. Photo by Elena E. Abrahamsson B.

to the Revolution (1933–1938), the Guardiola Building (1938–1941), the Hotel Reforma (1933), and the Pension Administration Building (1936), a project that was later modified, while still in design, to become the Hotel del Prado. (In the Hotel del Prado conversion project, Mario Pani made architectural interventions that gave rise to a grand—and in the end a more picturesque and trivial—polemic that ultimately created a strong enmity between the two men.)[2]

At the end of the 1940s Obregón won a competition for the Social Security Building (1946–1950), which was perhaps the last of his daring works. From this project until his death in 1961, he continued to be professionally active, but the depth of his involvement was unfortunately less, in comparison to the intense and profuse activity of his first twenty years of professional practice.

One of his most radical and notable characteristics is the skillful and constant presence of important connecting spaces between exterior and interior spaces in his buildings. This convergence between inside and outside gives his buildings an interesting and powerful urban scale. The buildings of Obregón Santacilia always make articulate entry conditions and transitions between public and private, anonymous and personal. The methods he utilizes to achieve this are varied, demonstrating his eclectic sensibility, his academic knowledge, and his mastery of the craft of architecture.

In the Ministry of Health Building (1925), for example, one enters across a large patio, where the internal circulation of the building is expressed with porticos, stairs, ramps, connecting bridges, and doorways. At the Hotel del Prado one enters into a large vestibule—in fact a succession of vestibules, two and three stories high—which are splendidly gradated as a spatial sequence from the street. The Guardiola Building offers two passages, which are a crossing of internal streets that act as urban connectors. In the Social Security Building, a large double-height portico is composed along the entire front facade and bears an empathetic relationship to the continuous row of trees on the Paseo de la Reforma. The Monument to the Revolution acts as a "gateway," an urban portal, and a pure space of transition.

Another significant characteristic of his work is the introduction of painting and sculpture in his buildings. With the frequent presence of sculpture—an antecedent to the discourses regarding *integración plástica* that were in vogue in the Ciudad Universitaria during the 1950s—we are able to observe that he worked more easily with sculpture than with color. In fact, Obregón Santacilia better understood the plasticity of volumes than that of surfaces. This is demonstrated by his natural inclination to integrate sculpture rather than painting in his architecture, in spite of the fact that Mexican painting of the time was much more developed and acclaimed than Mexican sculpture. The use of sculpture that we encounter in practically all his important buildings, particularly in his monuments, is always loose, relaxed, and fluid, and it is utilized as a fundamental component in his architectural language. Apart from this spontaneous affinity, it is possible that his academic background allowed him to recall and accept this relationship without major qualms. The work of Obregón Santacilia represents, perhaps, the last occurrence in twentieth-century Mexico of a systematic acceptance of a tradition that included sculptural elements as an integral part of architecture.

Obregón treats sculpture as an integral part of the composition, appearing as a natural continuation of the architectural volume. This fusion at a precise scale of the sculptural elements with the architecture is expressed in an integral relationship, not as a superimposed element. This is in contrast to the works of other architects, who used mural painting as superimposition, such as that which exists on both the inside and outside surfaces of the Ciudad Universitaria.

Obregón assigns a subordinate role to pictorial manifestations in his buildings. This is in contrast to the aggressive compositions

7.5. Carlos Obregón Santacilia, Instituto Mexicano del Seguro Social (Mexican Institute of Social Security Building), Mexico City, 1940. Photo by Edward R. Burian.

that characterize the Mexican Mural movement. Perhaps because of this sensibility, and in spite of the early collaboration with Diego Rivera for the murals and stained-glass windows for the Ministry of Health Building, one has to wait more than twenty years for the integration of the plastic arts to emerge as at the Ciudad Universitaria (where it at times dominates the architecture of the CU).

Obregón's command of scale allowed him to recognize the place of sculpture and painting in relation to architecture. One could argue that this treatment was already proclaimed by the principles of the orthodox academy and that this did not make a true contribution to the contemporary manifestation of the plastic arts. However, in spite of this, I believe that it is important and valuable to thoroughly explore the work of this fascinating architect. In addition to his use of orthodox principles, his language included the formal plastic vocabulary that emerged from the avant-garde that dominated his time.

The trajectory of his career represents a process of change and influences that corresponds—in general terms—to the historical period that changed the life of the country. After the Revolution, the country was eager to express its identity and find its cultural roots. However, this was difficult to realize, as the country's social and cultural conflicts were the product of the origins of Mexico itself: the violent blending of its Hispanic and indigenous peoples, of conquerors and conquered.

In addition, the growing influence of the United States, a foreign but powerful symbol of progress, pointed toward a technology and civilization that were *truly* modern. The European influence was primarily French, with the image of Paris as the seat of the grand artistic manifestations of *true* culture.

Obregón's academic formation caused him to realize works that followed rigorous, orthodox compositional principles, which he used correctly and skillfully. Simultaneously, he also explored the roots of historic nationalism. This was manifested in his more or less obvious references to the pre-Hispanic past and, more frequently, in his particular preference for models of colonial derivation. Frequently, he achieved rich and unusual forms by combining the language of historic nationalism with the Art Deco mode of composition. In other cases, his expression was openly contemporary, with reminiscences and quotations from Wagner, Perret, Mendelsohn, Oud, and Wright, as well as the simplified stylistic tendencies that appeared in Italian fascism.

Another significant aspect in the production of Obregón Santacilia was that the expressive and stylistic variety that took place during the first ten or fifteen years of his professional practice occurred simultaneously with a vast quantity of projects and realized works. What is unusual is that, in spite of his youth and the diversity of modes of composition that he utilized, upon analyzing each work as an independent composition, one doesn't see the superficial stylizations that one might expect to find. What one finds instead is the control and domain of a "craftsman," who utilized diverse principles in a confident manner without expressing any doubt regarding their validity.

Appearing in some of his last projects, assimilated and integrated in a personal mode, is an open recognition of the functional rationalism that was internationally in vogue and that established a truly contemporary Mexican vocabulary that ultimately became the dominant mode of composition.

The diverse influences and inconsistencies in the work of Carlos Obregón Santacilia suggest a characterization of his work as eclectic and unstable. In fact, his work is the product of a gradual discovery of a language that developed from a valid, clear-minded artistic vision. Every mutation of mode or style is a kind of voyage of discovery that includes new values without jettisoning past modes of composition—not merely the superficial and uncritical acceptance *per se* of these styles.

I believe that his decline in productivity during his mature years was not so much the consequence of his personal unwillingness. While I will not suggest direct causes, I believe it was the result of a frequent phenomenon that is little understood in our country. In the case of Obregón Santacilia (and many other architects in our country), his talents were diluted and wasted at the point in his career when he had established a significant presence with his creative ability, a time in an architect's life when he or she has finally accumulated the experience, wisdom, and capacity for synthesis.

When an architect such as Obregón Santacilia creates a prolific body of work that reflects a complex historical moment in Mexican culture, his production requires and merits a profound analysis, a careful investigation regarding its influences and a reevaluation of its characteristics, as much from the point of view of the path of his professional career as from its relationship to his academic foundations.

Carlos Obregón Santacilia created architecture that was at times heroic and nearly always monumental in scale. However, he also acknowledged his obligation to the city and understood that the design of individual buildings is *not* independent of the design of the city. He desired to celebrate both and also to make gentle interfaces between public and private domains with subtle transitions and significant connections.

He achieved the mastery of his craft and structured a language derived from the knowledge of historic styles, which he transformed and simplified in the face of contemporary architectural culture. In seeking to integrate the plastic arts within his architecture, he followed established principles of composition with regard to the conception of scale in relation to the entire work of architecture. Ultimately, his architecture was conceived in accordance with the predominant value of creating architecture on its own terms.

In light of this, few Mexican architects between the 1920s and 1940s have such varied, personal, and stimulating work as that of Carlos Obregón Santacilia.

Coyoacán, Mexico
January 1995

Notes

1. This chronology was taken from "La obra de Carlos Obregón Santacilia," by Graciela de Garay, *Cuadernos de Arquitectura y Conservación del Patrimonio Artístico 6.*
2. See Carlos Obregón Santacilia, *Historia folletinesca del Hotel del Prado.*

8   JUAN SEGURA

The Origins of Modern Architecture in Mexico

Antonio Toca Fernández

Translated by Edward R. Burian and Roberto Rodríguez

Introduction   The early works of Juan Segura (1898–1989), together with the work of other contemporary architects, marked the beginnings of Modern architecture in Mexico. While the architecture of Juan Segura in many respects disengaged itself from the academic practice that characterized the architecture of the Porfirio Díaz regime, it did not represent a radical and complete break from the past. Instead, it consciously embraced the formal vocabulary of traditional architectural language while utilizing the materials and technology of its time. This can be contrasted with the much more revolutionary transformation that was simultaneously occurring in the Mexican Mural movement—among artists such as Diego Rivera, David Alfaro Siqueiros, and José Clemente Orozco—which, for a variety of reasons, grew out of a more cohesive socio-cultural situation.

It is not the intent of this essay to define modernity, nor only to point to solitary protagonists such as Segura. One can only situate the work of Segura in his specific epoch, in which he acted as a distinguished practitioner who *did not* have an explicit theory and who only intended, somewhat modestly, to make a Mexican architecture appropriate to his time. Instead, this brief essay attempts to reintroduce his work to an audience that barely knows of his existence and to examine the "construction" of modern architectural history in Mexico by a generation of architectural historians who have relegated his work to one of transition. Understanding the various definitions that have been utilized in the past, the challenge is now to judge the importance of Segura's architectural production in relation to Modern Mexican architecture.

The built work of Segura was remarkable for its ability to engage a range of architectural issues during a period of rapid change in post-Revolutionary Mexico. The resolution of contemporary architectural programs of the 1930s resulted in the creation of new types of spatial organization for individual buildings, which *also* responded to the larger order of the urban design of the city. Innovative tectonic solutions for materials and their assembly, including carpentry, ironwork, light fixtures, decoration, finishes, and the creative use of color, were integrated into his work. Very innovative solutions to technical systems, including mechanical and electrical systems, were incorporated into

8.1. Juan Segura, Ermita Building, doorway at lobby, Mexico City, 1930–1931. Photo by Edward R. Burian.

each of his projects. Finally, he attempted to link his architecture with an ongoing Mexican artistic tradition, modernizing it in relation to the available resources of the time.

Segura and the Escuela de Bellas Artes

Juan Segura was born in Mexico City in 1898. He received his architectural education at the Escuela de Bellas Artes (School of Fine Arts) at the Academy of San Carlos from 1917 to 1921. The evolution of Segura's work offers an insight into the didactic and ideological context of the Escuela de Bellas Artes. His work was an example—in practice—of the critical pedagogical principles in which he was schooled. The method of composition, the skill and creativity of drawing, the careful concern for the *ensemble* of the building and its details, the attention to decoration (which was not yet prohibited), and the amazing ability to utilize new systems of construction were characteristic of the skills Segura inherited from his schooling.

Post-Revolutionary Culture and the Continuity of Tradition

The consolidation of the post-Revolutionary state began slowly with the economic recovery of the country. The activation of economic processes began in the second half of the decade of the 1920s. Within this economic context, construction activity had practically ceased. The architects who taught classes at the Academy of San Carlos were no more than thirty in number and were little more than students themselves.[1] The cultural transformation demanded by the Mexican Revolution was created with the improvised program of the newly appointed minister of education, José Vasconcelos. His support for the activities of muralists, painters, writers, and musicians was crucial to fill the void represented by the antiquated aesthetics of the deposed *porfirista* regime. However, this new cultural vision antagonized the powerful elitist classes that supported a Eurocentric cultural construct. Generally, the architects of the time were more identified with the recently overthrown dictatorship than with the triumphant revolutionaries! This was the reason why, for the most part, the architecture of the first years of the twenties in many respects conserved the formal characteristics of the deposed regime.

Because of the incapacity of professional architects and academics to offer new formal solutions for the post-Revolutionary state, a new generation of students offered an alternative vision. The graduates of the first years of the 1920s began this transformation, with Carlos Obregón Santacilia, José Villagrán García, Enrique del Moral, Vicente Mendiola, Carlos Tarditi, and Juan Segura among the most well known. However, the break with the tradition in which they were educated was neither easy nor rapid. The few architectural commissions that existed were in the private sector and were primarily private homes or apartments. The early post-Revolutionary government did not possess a clear cultural agenda that supported innovation; instead, the simplistic but powerful culture of the Porfiriato dominated.

The colonial religious architecture that Vasconcelos believed was the fountain of formal inspiration did not constitute a radical break with tradition. Instead, it was a more appropriate continuation of the practice of the École de Beaux Arts in terms of the stylistic manipulation of architecture. Modern architecture was not intended in principle to completely break with past models without substituting other more culturally appropriate models. The aggressiveness that characterized the movements in painting and sculpture, with the support of Vasconcelos, did not apply to the activity of architecture. The first works of Obregón Santacilia and Villagrán García reflected the profound influence of the Academy, in the sense that its traditional models were utilized. The National Lottery Building (1924) was a specific example of this phenomenon. Subsequent works such as the National Stadium by Villagrán (1924) and the Benito Juárez School of Obregón Santacilia (1925) were examples of the utilization of elements of colonial architecture in their composition.[2]

New Programs: The Ermita, Isabel, and Eugenia Buildings

One of the characteristics most evident in Segura's work was his particular transformation and creation of architectural programs. His work for the Mier and Pesado Foundation from 1926 to 1935 was interesting in that the projects were driven by the notion of the maximum profit for the minimum investment.[3] Within these constraints Segura proposed bold and innovative solutions, and the example of the Ermita Building (1930–1931) was particularly noteworthy. The proposed siting, together with the advantage of two front facades—one on Avenida Revolución and another on Avenida Jalisco—helped to define the importance of these streets. For Avenida Revolución, a new urban type was created with the geometry of the Ermita Building. This solution maintained the traditional private court, which was also used in the Isabel complex. For practical reasons, commercial functions were incorporated on the two public facades in each building. Apartments of

8.2. Juan Segura, Ermita Building, exterior view looking south, Mexico City, 1930–1931. Courtesy of the Giffords Collection, taken in the early 1930s.

8.3. Juan Segura, Ermita Building, exterior view looking south, Mexico City. Photo by Edward R. Burian, taken in June 1995.

one, two, and three bedrooms were situated on the upper floors above the commercial functions. The apartments were favorably oriented to face Avenida Revolución. The beautifully articulated private entryways for pedestrians were typical compositional themes of Segura.

The modernization and transformation of the architectural program was one of the most dramatic interventions in the design solution of the Ermita Building. Segura incorporated a zone of commercial use on the ground floor, one- and two-bedroom apartments on the upper floors, and sandwiched in between these floors, a cinema that ingeniously utilized the triangular geometry of the site. This scheme created a triple-height interior court that collected the circulation of the various apartments.

The massing of the building on the acute triangular site terminates the view from the Avenida Tacubaya. The scheme contained

8.4. *Juan Segura, Ermita Building, exterior view looking north, Mexico City, 1930–1931. Photo by Edward R. Burian.*

a bank on the lower level as well as an entrance lobby with elevators and the stairs. With a modest, traditional formal vocabulary and a bold strategy for spatial organization, it was in 1930 a multifunctional building that was actually built prior to the proposals of Le Corbusier for the Marseille Unité.[4] Clearly, it was a modern solution to an equally modern program.

Rationalization and Spatial Distribution

The innovation of the architectural programs also extended to the spatial organization of the interiors. The modern attitude expressed in the general functional organization of the building was also manifested in the innovative design of particular functions. For example, throughout his career, Segura sought to cen-

8.5. Juan Segura, Ermita Building, view at interior court, Mexico City, 1930–1931. Photo by Edward R. Burian.

tralize the services of the building, including baths and kitchens, as well as to design patios with natural light for illumination and ventilation, which can be seen in the Isabel (1929–1930), Eugenia (1930), and Ermita (1930–1931) Buildings.

The solution for the plumbing and mechanical systems, which included natural gas, was rationalized and collected in a precise manner on roofs and patios to achieve a more economical means of construction and easier maintenance. He also gave careful attention to the design of the exterior facades as well as patios, gardens, paving, and decorative details.

New Construction

Materials

When the problem permitted, Segura utilized his particular design sensibility to provide innovative construction solutions. His period of professional activity parallels the inception, at the industrial level, of the use of cement in building construction in Mexico. However, its utilization in building construction required a concerted effort on the part of Segura in order to overcome the public's reticence and lack of confidence regarding the material. From the beginning of his career, Segura utilized reinforced concrete in roof and beam design and in construction details for basements and stairs, as well as in the finished claddings of artificial granite and colored stone.

Segura's use of structural steel was not its first occurrence in Mexico, as the principal buildings of the Porfiriato utilized this structural system. However, in the case of the Ermita Building, the additional weight of three floors of apartments above the cinema necessitated the innovative use of structural steel. This was extraordinarily daring for the time if we consider that in the first part of the 1930s there was no precedent he could look to for a solution to this problem.

A project that is especially interesting for both its modesty and originality is the Elderly Care Facility in Orizaba. Because of the lack of industrialized materials and the high cost to obtain them, Segura creatively utilized a traditional brick and roof structure with *vigas* of wood and a sloping tile roof.

The Importance

of Ornament

One of the qualities most evident in the work of Segura was the extraordinary care in designing ornament. This was precisely because it takes into account the cultural necessity of ornament, which was not yet considered "a crime" in Mexico.[5] It is possible to observe that there was a definite tendency in his mature work to overcome the decorativeness and picturesqueness of his earliest neo-Colonial revival work, and in the case of the Isabel Building, to create a more abstract and sober architecture. Segura did not acquiesce to the scenographic interpretation of colonial architecture. On the contrary, he utilized ornament in a subtle manner that was an *integral* part of the building, as opposed to merely decoration. For example, functional organization, structural bays, and the identification of housing units were rationally demarcated on the facades. This produced an aesthetic that was comprehensible and accessible to all, and permitted the newly conceived incorporation of traditional symbols.

8.6. Juan Segura, Isabel Building, exterior view from street, Mexico City, 1929–1930. Photo by Edward R. Burian.

8.7. Juan Segura, Isabel Building, view of interior court, Mexico City, 1929–1930. Photo by Edward R. Burian.

An Economical

and Well-Crafted

Mexican

Architecture

Segura's central preoccupation, as well as that of the rest of his colleagues in the difficult post-Revolutionary era, was to make an architecture that responded to Mexico's culture and that was economical and well built. He gradually achieved this by changing the functional and formal organization of his architecture. Even a cursory review of the plans of his buildings makes this gradual transformation evident.

Significantly, the efficient utilization of economic, technical, and constructive resources was manifested by the variety and quality of Segura's work. The fact that individual clients and institutions were hesitant to commit scarce capital to risky ventures represents the difficult *reality* of professional practice in the post-Revolutionary period. In particular, Segura's direct involvement in the business aspects of architecture reassured his clients during this volatile time. Sensitive to the problems of living, health, recreation, and the access to services, Segura offered a dignified response in his buildings for the Mier y Pesado Foundation. In his more anonymous work for constructors and developers, he created an architectural response that possessed many more qualities than just meeting the minimum requirements for mere financial speculation.

Segura and the

"Construction"

of a History

of Modern

Architecture

in Mexico

Frequently, the work of Segura is labeled as Art Deco, a term he himself ignored until 1978. This does an unequivocal injustice to his work in relation to his contemporaries, for it in fact comprises the beginnings of Modern architecture in Mexico and is of enormous importance in terms of Mexican culture.[6]

To locate the work of Juan Segura within the development of Mexican architecture yields a particularly interesting result. His architectural activity, culminating in the 1940s, constitutes a body of work that is notable for its quantity and quality. However, the work has generally been considered an outstanding example of what is usually termed an architecture of transition, and it has been erroneously called Art Deco.[7]

Once a more schematic and abstract version of the Modern movement was accepted—a notion that gained ascendancy in Mexico in the 1950s—several misconceptions emerged. The Porfirio Díaz era was perceived as having been dominated by the influence of European culture, and modernity was equated with the docile copying of international architecture. All architecture situated between these two periods was considered one of transition.

This overly schematic classification resulted in an enormous indifference to both the architects and the works situated in this period.[8] In this version of history, the work of Segura and other architects is only an interesting example of Mexican Art Deco, and is considered, in an overly simplistic manner, an anachronistic example of protomodernism.[9] However, this model does not clarify the different revivals that occurred in Mexico prior to the arrival of "Modern architecture."

A Heterogeneous and Contradictory Modern Movement

It is both interesting and revealing that the period of the most open embracing of international Functionalism in Mexico—the decade of the 1950s—acknowledged that this movement was not homogeneous and that there were diverse variants. This development was not merely coincidental but corresponded precisely with the well-orchestrated propaganda that began to impose itself by the adoption in Mexico of the models of the "international" Modern movement, particularly those of Walter Gropius and Ludwig Mies van der Rohe. Post-Revolutionary architectural production before rationalism was simply forgotten, or in the best case, regarded as schematic.

Figures such as Juan Segura, Juan O'Gorman, Juan Legarreta, Alvaro Aburto, Francisco Serrano, and Carlos Tarditi were ignored by historians for many years, and only with the crisis of the Modern movement was there an effort to resurrect these figures. A different situation existed in regard to Villagrán García, Del Moral, Obregón Santacilia, Yáñez, and Barragán. These architects were not jettisoned by history due to the fact that they produced architecture continuously throughout their careers. The buildings of these architects were radically transformed in the forties, as their designers gradually distanced themselves from the full range of Le Corbusier's contemporaneous ideas of the time and substituted a progressively more abstract conception of Modern architecture.

Art Deco: An Ambiguous Term

The ambiguity of the term "Art Deco" embodies many different formal characteristics. In fact, its utilization since the 1960s reflects the intent of a "revival," like the one that occurred with Art Nouveau. Without a doubt, the European architectural production of the twenties has a variety of different formal characteristics that coexist with the Moderne, which was later definitively called Art Deco. After 1925, with the Exposition Internationale des Arts Décoratifs et Industriels Modernes (Exposition of Decorative Arts) in Paris, we are best able to understand this convergence of buildings with these specific formal characteristics, yet with individual differences between them.[10] If one carefully analyzes the production of what has been called Art Deco, these fundamental differences can be established. From the first part of the century, other architects such as Otto Wagner, Josef Hoffman, Joseph Maria Olbrich, Auguste Perret, and Tony Garnier had already formally broken with the eclectic tradition of the École de Beaux Arts, creating buildings that were distancing themselves from the Art Nouveau.

This distinction is fundamental, and until now, the explanations of the Art Deco in Mexico do not acknowledge this aspect. With the Exposition of Decorative Arts in 1925, this architectural production was relegated to the limbo of a transitional period or a stylistic phenomenon. The triumph of rationalism helped to consolidate this explanation because it became evident that with the break from the model of the Beaux Arts, all of the production realized before the ascendancy of rationalism was considered, after the fact, a transition or proto-modern. It is very important to clarify this progressive transformation that was manifested in Mexico from 1920 onward regarding the formal criteria used in other very important buildings and projects that exemplify this approach to modernity.

The Diverse Modernisms

The difference between what was considered modern in 1937 in Esther Born's book, and the definition in 1956—almost twenty years later—demonstrates how the radical Functionalism of the thirties, in counter distinction with the "decent" and "glossy" Functionalism of the fifties, conforms with the official version of the Modern movement. From this point, this substitution proceeded to forget the more antagonistic version of the avant-garde, and in the best of cases, to draw a "suspicious smile" when referring to the so-called "masters of the modern movement."[11]

Despite the fact that Juan Segura was branded an Art Deco architect, he was not conscious that he belonged to a specific movement. His only ambition was to make modern architecture linked to the historical tradition of his country.[12] One could make the point that the characterization of Segura as an Art Deco architect is unfair and inexact, and the examination of his buildings allows us to appreciate his talent, and interestingly, his modern position. If one is open to understanding that the modernity of the 1930s is different, for diverse reasons, than our understanding of it fifty years later . . . then one can see that Segura's work was indeed modern.

Conclusion

Ultimately, it is possible to acknowledge that the largely unknown work of Segura, contemporary with the work of Tarditi, Legarreta, and Yáñez, deserves greater critical attention. His innovative responses in terms of program, formal and functional organization, materials, tectonics, and sensuous qualities need to be reconsidered in light of the decadence and ignorance that in many cases produced the anonymous "International Style" in Mexico and many other countries.

Before hurriedly beginning the task of the recovery of postmodern historic styles, we must reevaluate the work of Segura and of other protagonists of Modern Mexican architecture. In this regard, it is important to recall that if we do not remember and value the past, we will not to be able to have a responsible and dignified future.

Segura's work merits more careful study. His work was a simple and creative response, full of commonsense solutions for the problems generated in Mexico City of the early 1930s.[13]

Notes

1. Discussed in an interview with Juan Segura in *Cuadernos de Arquitectura* 15\16, Mexico City: INBA, 1981.

2. See I. Katzman's book *La arquitectura contemporánea mexicana.*

3. The Mier y Pesados Foundation's main goal was to make a prudent, profitable investment. Segura's buildings were remarkable not only for their quality but also for their economy.

4. Segura's Ermita Building was completed in 1931 and was an interesting example of a multifunctional program. Le Corbusier's *Unités* were not built until the 1940s.

5. In Adolf Loos's article "Ornament and Crime," "primitive" cultures are portrayed as utilizing ornament in their buildings and artifacts, while "refined" cultures eliminate ornament and thus do not commit artistic "crimes."

6. In an interview, Segura acknowledged that he ignored the term "Art Deco" until the late 1970s. During the 1930s in Mexico there were different stylistic definitions in architecture such as "Moderne," "Zig-Zag," and "Streamline" among others.

7. A posteriori, the work of Segura has been erroneously defined as Art Deco because, at the triumph of rationalism, all other approaches to Modern architecture were labeled as architecture of "transition."

8. Only recently has there been an attempt to evaluate the work of architects such as Juan Segura, Francisco Serrano, and Carlos Obregón Santacilia.

9. The term "Modern architecture" was applied only to works that clearly were linked to the rationalism of Le Corbusier, such as those of Juan O'Gorman.

10. The publications of the Exposition Internationale des Arts Décoratifs et Industriels Modernes clearly showed that there were many definitions of what was understood as modernity. Some buildings were more "stylistic" and ornamented than others. In Segura's case, his work was abstract and geometric, linked more with the forms of the Viennese Secession than with picturesque ornamentalism or with the rationalism of Le Corbusier.

11. The historical account of Modern architecture has suffered many misunderstandings and exaggerations, especially in the "mythological" works of Sir Nikolaus Pevsner and Sigfried Giedion on the "master builders." With the dissemination of the work of other critics, the real and controversial history emerged, and the heroes and villains of the "mythological" versions were situated in a more objective perspective.

12. Interview with Juan Segura, *Cuadernos de Arquitectura* 15–16, Mexico City: INBA/SEP, and numerous personal conversations with him over the years.

13. For further elaboration on this subject, see A. Toca Fernández, *Juan Segura: Orígenes de la arquitectura moderna en México*.

9   THE ARCHITECTURE AND URBANISM

OF MARIO PANI

Creativity and Compromise

Louise Noelle Merles

Translated by Edward R. Burian and José Carlos Fernández

Introduction

Mario Pani stands out as one of the most prolific and original architects of twentieth-century Mexico. His projects and built works, which span a sixty-year career, reflect a creative search into diverse areas of architectural practice. The relevance of his proposals and the quality of his constructed work are significant contributions to architectural culture and mark him as one of the major protagonists of the Modern movement.

Unfortunately, Pani's work is largely unknown outside of Mexico, particularly to an English-speaking audience. In this context, the focus of this essay is to provide a brief overview of this prolific architect's individual buildings and urban design proposals and to survey his vital contribution to the development in Mexico of urban multifamily housing that included the integration of public art.

Background and Early Projects

This unique man was born in Mexico City on March 29, 1911,[1] at the dawn of a new era in which Mexico was emerging as a modern country. Early in his childhood, he moved to Europe with his father, Arturo Pani, a diplomat for Mexico. His experience in postwar Italy and his education at the École de Beaux Arts in Paris gave him a rich background in cultural traditions. In June of 1934 he was able to obtain first place in the entry examination to the Beaux Arts architecture school from over six hundred applicants.

A few months later, he validated his European degree at the Escuela Nacional de Arquitectura [National School of Architecture] at the UNAM in Mexico City. At this point in his life, he relocated to the city of his birth and immediately reintegrated himself back into the productive life of Mexico. The young architect found fertile ground for his creative proposals, as his return coincided with the incipient economic development and nascent industrialization of the country, particularly in the construction industry. In this way, he was able to offer novel solutions that also responded to the diverse requirements of each project. This ambitious Mexican architect was able to integrate his European experience with the concerns of Mexican architecture of the time, in particular, the theoretical propositions advocated by José Villagrán García at the National School of Architecture. The results were designs that benefited from his exposure to both of these academic traditions in terms of solutions appropriate to the problems of the time, but that also found distinct expressions at a number of levels. These ranged from investigations into materials and technical issues to questions of form and meaning in an attempt to produce a vocabulary that responded to specific functions.

The first works of Pani reveal compositional strategies in which the academic precepts of the Beaux Arts prevail. He treats these buildings as pronounced axial compositions, with carefully organized functions and a tendency toward the monumental. Even in these early projects, diverse works of visual art are combined and integrated with decidedly modern materials. This is manifested in the Hotel Reforma, designed barely a year after his return from Europe; in the Hotel Alameda in Morelia, Michoacán, in 1938; and in the Hotel Plaza in 1946 in Mexico City, where the curve again plays a preponderant part in the design. Other buildings of the period are characterized by their formal innovation and functional resolution, including the Escuela Nacional de Maestros [National Teachers College] and, a year later, the Conservatorio Nacional de Música [National Conservatory of Music], where the art programs for the buildings were executed by José Clemente Orozco, Luis Ortiz Monasterio, and Armando Quezada.

Pani's efforts to solve diverse problems of the country at the time, such as those related to health, led to the realization of the Hospitals for Tuberculosis in Perote, Veracruz; Saltillo, Coahuila; and Tulancingo, Hidalgo, in the first years of the 1940s. Pani was also involved in the Plan Nacional de Hospitales [National Hospital Plan] that culminated in the Centro Médico Nacional [National Medical Center] project, in collaboration with José Villagrán García.[2]

A series of apartment buildings realized between 1944 and 1946, which featured innovative solutions for the internal distri-

9.1. Mario Pani, National Conservatory of Music, Mexico City, 1946. Photo courtesy of the Archive of Louise Noelle Merles.

bution of functions, were antecedents for the development of his multifamily housing projects. Pani was also interested in the rationalization of urban growth. The densification of new construction could potentially provide beneficial services to the user as well as be cost-effective in terms of the utilization of the infrastructure of the city.

The *Multifamiliares* [Multifamily Housing Projects] In 1947, the assistant director of Civil Pensions, Lic. José de Jesús Lima, solicited Mario Pani for a proposal for two hundred single-family housing units on a site of 40,000 square meters, located at the intersection of Avenidas Coyoacán and Félix Cuevas in Mexico City. In addressing this problem, Pani and his design team produced a preliminary scheme that persuaded the directors of this organization of the necessity to change the use of the land and its density to relieve the burgeoning population of the city.

9.2. Mario Pani, aerial view of President Alemán Urban Housing Project, Mexico City, 1949. Photo courtesy of the Archive of Louise Noelle Merles.

Their solution proposed the construction of one thousand multifamily apartments on the same site. Moreover, with the collaboration of the engineer Bernardo Quintana, who founded Ingenieros Civiles Asociados [ICA; Associated Civil Engineers], a study was presented that demonstrated the feasibility of this scheme, as it could be built for the same amount of money originally budgeted for the two hundred single-family units! In this manner, and against the cultural preference of Mexicans to possess a low-scale *casita*, the first group of high-density multifamily housing, the Centro Urbano Presidente Alemán [President Alemán Urban Housing Project], was constructed between 1947 and 1949. The term *multifamiliares* was coined for this type of multifamily housing in Mexico, which also featured the separation of the pedestrian and the automobile in the superblock.[3]

In the President Alemán Urban Housing Project, the strategy was to adopt a system of architecture and urbanism of tall buildings distributed in a manner that left the ground plane free for gardens and areas of relaxation. In addition, Pani conveniently allocated zones of social service, with child care centers or pools, and zones of commercial services. The final scheme contained six buildings of thirteen stories, four of which were organized in a zig-zag manner following the diagonal pattern of the site, which

9.3. Mario Pani, view of multistory housing, President Alemán Urban Housing Project, Mexico City, 1949. Photo courtesy of the Archive of Louise Noelle Merles. offered an optimal eastern orientation for all apartments. Six buildings of only three stories each completed the project. This resulted in the development of apartments with two levels, which allowed for the privacy of the bedrooms, and made possible the placement of subdividing partitions in accordance with the needs of each tenant. This strategy allowed for a circulation corridor to occur only once for every three floors, which reduced the construction cost of the elevator system. Significantly, the finished surfaces of exposed concrete and brick, which were initially economic choices, ultimately proved easy to maintain.

It is important to consider this project in relation to Le Corbusier's proposals for housing. Undoubtedly, they were a fountain of inspiration for Pani, who had attended the revolutionary conferences of the Swiss master during his studies in Paris. It is also important to recall that he knew firsthand the principles of the Ville Radieuse (1946–1952) and probably also knew the Marseilles Unité scheme, which was completed three years after the President Alemán Urban Housing Project. However, it should be emphasized that Pani's project did not merely copy Le Corbusier's scheme but was instead based on his own ideas for denser urbanism and took special account of the *modus vivendi* of Mexicans. In this sense, techniques and materials were adapted to local conditions, which differed from those in France. In addition, the floor plans responded to the necessities of a family in the city, with bedrooms on one level and kitchen and dining room on another. This is in contrast to the units at Marseilles, which were primarily developed on a single floor but with double-height living rooms and an interior corridor circulation system from the elevators. The quality and success of Pani's solutions are clearly reflected in their users' acceptance through the years.

Public Art in the Multifamily Housing Projects

Pani's concern to integrate diverse arts in his work was realized by the economic rationalization of construction, which allowed enough remaining funds to invite José Clemente Orozco to paint murals as a collaborator. The noted *tapatío* painter began a mural entitled *La primavera* (The Spring) on one undulating wall especially constructed for the purpose, but the painting was never completed because of the artist's sudden and unexpected death. Carlos Mérida also collaborated with a frieze and various figures for the child care center, of which little has survived.

A few years later, the Centro Urbano Presidente Juárez [President Juárez Urban Housing Project] (1950–1952; Salvador Ortega, Associate Architect) presents a more resolved solution that attempts to overcome the aggressiveness conferred by certain materials, and that features more variation in the design of the dwelling units. The variety of apartment units responds to the diverse sizes of families. Twelve different types of units are offered in four different sizes of buildings: one of thirteen floors, five of ten floors, four of seven floors, and nine of four floors. Given the large area of the site (which also contains a public park), the apartment buildings are distributed so that every unit receives adequate sunlight and is sited to avoid shadows cast by

9.4. *Mario Pani, view of President Juárez Urban Housing Project, with inset sculpture panels by Carlos Mérida, Mexico City, 1950–1952; partially destroyed in the 1985 earthquake. Photo courtesy of the Archive of Louise Noelle Merles.*

adjacent structures. At the same time, the diverse civic services, schools, and commercial functions that were projected favor a self-sufficient *unidad habitacional* [housing project]. Other characteristics of the project are the preservation of the integrity of the site so that pedestrians are able to walk without the danger of automobiles. In this spirit, the Avenida Orizaba is allowed to pass below four of the buildings. Automobile access is resolved along the periphery by means of a restricted roadway that gives access to the parking.

It should be noted that this proposal also featured the integration of public art in the form of low-relief murals of concrete executed by the Guatemalan painter Carlos Mérida. These pre-Hispanic–inspired designs are found on some buildings and occur on the exterior walls of closets, on the roofs, or on the exterior stairs, where the priests from the past eternally climb the stairs of modern "temples." The art also included the mural *Juego de Niños* in the child care center and a series of abstract elements on the automobile underpass of the building, visible to passing automobiles. A unique result is attained by combining concrete, that ubiquitous twentieth-century material, with the creativity nourished by the legends and codices of the pre-Columbian world. "Art of the future, without political demagoguery, but eminently universal. Art for the masses, public art for the view of all, for the emotional enjoyment of the whole world,"[4] is how the artist defines his work, which on this occasion creates an "extraordinarily beautiful integration."[5]

9.5. *Mario Pani, view of President Juárez Urban Housing Project open stair, with low relief by Carlos Mérida, Mexico City, 1950–1952. Photo courtesy of the Archive of Louise Noelle Merles.*

This work was probably one of the strongest examples of *integración plástica,* a movement that was especially popular in the 1950s and that was in large part a reaction by architects to the abstraction and repetitiveness of the so-called International Style, which ignored the specific qualities of individual cultures. Reflecting their concern for the particularities of place, some architects sought to integrate works of local art with a nationalistic inclination into their buildings. This practice did not consist of mere adornment; rather, it represented a real collaboration between architects and artists in search of a congruent result, not only in

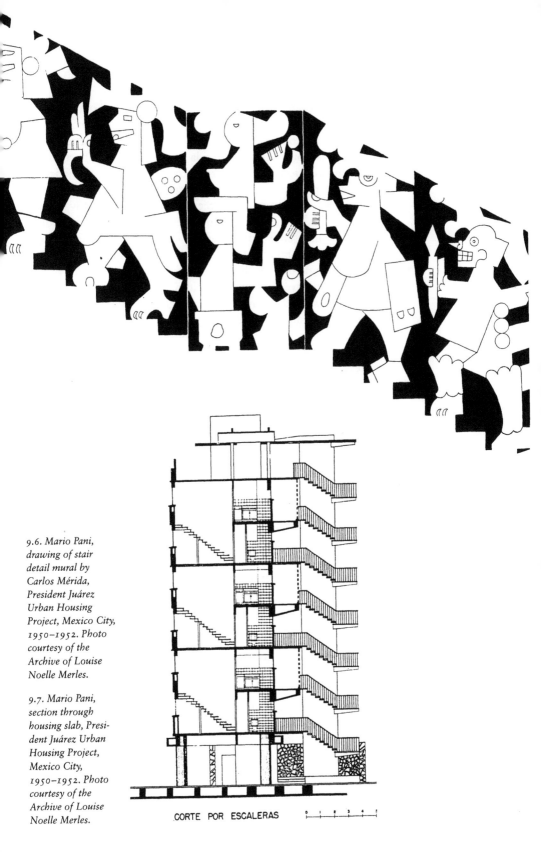

9.6. Mario Pani, drawing of stair detail mural by Carlos Mérida, President Juárez Urban Housing Project, Mexico City, 1950–1952. Photo courtesy of the Archive of Louise Noelle Merles.

9.7. Mario Pani, section through housing slab, President Juárez Urban Housing Project, Mexico City, 1950–1952. Photo courtesy of the Archive of Louise Noelle Merles.

CORTE POR ESCALERAS

185

spirit but also in form. This was accomplished without abandoning the precepts of Modern architecture. While some painters proposed a stronger emphasis on social issues, the best results, as in the case of Pani and Mérida, evolved from a harmonious working relationship that strove to resolve both aesthetic and technical problems. The artists' proclivity to produce abstract murals helped earn popular acceptance for an art that was accessible to the public yet could be integrated with a contemporary building. In a sense, this movement relates to the Bauhaus proposition of the total communion of the arts, as well as to Le Corbusier's mural designs that were directly cast into concrete. However, in the development of this idea in Mexico, the approach is overlaid with the particular iconography and sensibilities of Mexican culture and tradition.

In regard to multifamily dwellings, it is necessary to mention other proposals by Mario Pani for the solution of housing in Mexico, such as the Multifamiliar para Maestros en la Ciudad Universitaria [Multifamily Housing for University Faculty; 1951–1952], as well as the Unidad Habitacional Santa Fe del Instituto Mexicano del Seguro Social [Santa Fe Housing Project of the Mexican Social Security Institute; 1953–1954], which consists of a return to urbanization by means of the single-family residence. The culmination of his experience in the field of housing resulted in the Ciudad Habitacional Nonoalco-Tlatelolco [Nonoalco-Tlatelolco Urban Housing Project; 1960–1964], with a capacity for more than 100,000 inhabitants. This complex was planned as a *barrio* interspersed with commercial space, schools, and recreation space. In this dense urban scheme Pani proposed apartments for diverse economic classes, with living areas for distinct types of families. Automobile circulation was organized on the periphery with only restricted penetration inside the site to handle parking.

Mario Pani also promoted the Ley de Condominios [Condominium Law], which permitted a substantial modification of the lifestyle of many Mexicans. He also erected the first condominium in the capital city along its principal avenue, the Paseo de la Reforma, and later, the Condominium Los Cocos in 1956 in Acapulco, Guerrero, where he had built various vacation residences and a yacht club in 1955.

It is also important to point out that Pani associated with a number of colleagues, and that in the majority of these collaborations, his style and personality prevailed: a contemporary European expression based on the principles of Functionalism.

9.8. Mario Pani, Nonoalco-Tlatelolco Urban Housing Project, aerial view, Mexico City, 1964. Photo courtesy of the Archive of Louise Noelle Merles.

Without a doubt, the development of his plastic solutions was extended by the existence of his large atelier, which responded to the various demands of professional practice.

Of the diverse associations established by Pani, one of the most prolonged and prolific was that maintained with Enrique del Moral. The results of this collaboration included the buildings for the Secretaría de Recursos Hidráulicos [Ministry of Hydraulic Resources; 1950] in Mexico City, several hotels and houses, as well as the airport and the Plaza de Toros [bullring] in the port of Acapulco, realized between 1950 and 1955. A better-known project is the Master Plan for the Ciudad Universitaria and the building design for the Rector's Tower, which was inaugurated in 1952. Their association on the Ciudad Universitaria resulted in one of the great works of Mexican architecture, where, under the direction of these two men, more than 150 architects and artists collaborated to produce an environment that represented both a culmination of the modern era and a door to the second half of our century.

Among the noteworthy professional activities of Mario Pani was his involvement in planning and urbanization as head of the Taller de Urbanismo [Urbanism Workshop], in which José Luis Cuevas and Domingo García Ramos also had important roles. He participated in the master plans for the Ciudad Universitaria and the Ciudad Satélite, as well as the planning on a larger scale for Acapulco, Guerrero; Guaymas, Sonora; and Mazatlán, Sinaloa; the regional plan of Yucatán; and the studies for the Plan Nacional Fronterizo along the border, which evaluated cities such as Matamoros, Tamaulipas; Piedras Negras, Coahuila; and Ciudad Juárez, Chihuahua—all of which demonstrate the scale of his proposals over the decades of the fifties and sixties. His concerns for rational planning, which focused on future development, were unfortunately canceled or modified by the succeeding presidential administrations and were realized only as piecemeal accretions.

Pani was also instrumental in defining and promoting Modern architecture, influencing numerous students in his course on composition between 1940 and 1948 at the Escuela Nacional de Arquitectura at the UNAM and later at the Universidad Anáhuac, as well as those that worked in his studio. At the same time, he was involved in the discussion of formative ideas in his profession by editing the magazine *Arquitectura/México* for more than forty years, from 1938 to 1979. Through the magazine he allowed Mexican architects to expose their work to the architectural media beyond national borders, into the international arena. In its 119 volumes, the value and development of the discipline was recorded, and the magazine remains an invaluable fountain of information. His profound interest in the architectural profession motivated him to create the Academia Nacional de Arquitectura [National Academy of Architecture] in 1978, and brought him recognition in the form of numerous awards, including the Premio Nacional de Artes in 1986, before his death on February 23, 1993.

Mario Pani was an innovator and creator known beyond the architectural arena whose importance lies in his ideas and proposals with respect to the practice of his profession. This architect was able to offer both functional and novel responses to the various problems he encountered in the public and private sector. Without a doubt, the importance of his works does not lie in the novelty of forms and materials but in his concepts and solutions that addressed the specifics of his time and the particularities of place, and established a respected position for him within the realm of international architecture.

Notes

1. For this and other subsequent facts, see Manuel Larrosa's *Mario Pani: Arquitecto de su época,* pp. 119–123, and my own essay "Mario Pani" in *Arquitectos contemporáneos de México.*

2. The then-recently founded magazine *Arquitectura/México* demonstrates the extent of this program in Mexico in its April 1944 issue, Number 15.

3. Mario Pani's book *Los multifamiliares de pensiones* offers a review of this complex as well as the Centro Urbano Presidente Juárez and the Multifamiliar para Maestros en la Ciudad Universitaria, explaining the author's proposals.

4. Carlos Mérida, from the prologue of a catalog of the exhibition of his work.

5. See Mathías Goeritz's article "La integración plástica en el C. U. Presidente Juárez," in Mario Pani's *Los multifamiliares de pensiones,* pp. 101–108. The relevance and quality of this example make its destruction all the more sad, attributable as it is, not to the earthquake of September 19, 1985, but to a lack of aesthetic conscience on the part of the administrators who were in charge.

POSTSCRIPT

Guadalajara . . . Guadalajara . . .
The smell of the undefiled damp earth . . .

— *Words from a traditional Mexican folk song*

Up- and downhill we went, but always descending. We had
left the hot wind behind and were sinking into pure, airless heat.
The stillness seemed to be waiting for something.

— *Juan Rulfo,* Pedro Páramo

As this postscript is being written (March 1995), dramatic and rapid changes have occurred in Mexico. Within the past six months, the world has been shocked by the assassinations of the PRI presidential candidate Luis Colosio, and the executive secretary of the PRI, Francisco Ruiz Massieu. President Ernesto Zedillo has taken office in the midst of the tumult of the peso devaluation, civil unrest in Chiapas, and serious accusations of impropriety involving the previous administration. These events will seriously challenge the trajectory of modernity as a national ideology and threaten technological modernization as a national project. The reality of the current economic crisis will have a profound impact upon the means by which architects, among others, realize their work.

In this context, a book entitled *Modernity and the Architecture of Mexico* may seem little more than an aesthetic exercise. While this book attempts to raise critical issues and provide insight into the phenomenon of modernity and its particular manifestation in regard to the architecture of Mexico, these are more than merely interesting insights. They present an argument for the serious material implications of architectural production. The actions of a generation that has preceded ours provoke many questions with regard to critical practice for our challenging times.

1. Has the project of modernity ended in Mexico and elsewhere, or is it still an ongoing enterprise?
2. Is what we do as architects an autonomous aesthetic practice, or does meaning arise out of the social, cultural, and climatic experience of place?
3. Given the current economic and ecological realities in Mexico,

how should one build? Could the confrontation of these realities ultimately result in a richer, more meaningful architecture
that engages labor, systems of production, materials and their
assembly, and tectonic order?

It is my hope that these essays provoke this kind of ongoing discussion. However, the answer to these questions is beyond the
scope of this postscript and is another book in itself.

Several specific observations can be made and questions raised
from the essays. While virtually none of the existing texts on
Modern Mexican architecture (which are primarily a chronological listing of works) confront the ideological issues of modernity,
almost all the introductions of these books portray or imply a
vague connection between an emerging progressive future and
Mexico's pre-Hispanic past. The implicit conclusion is that Mex-

10.1. *Luis Barragán, house for two families on Avenida Parque, Mexico City, 1936.
Photo by Edward R. Burian, taken in June 1995.*

10.2. *Luis Barragán, ruin of garden of El Pedregal, Mexico City, 1945–1950.
Photo by Edward R. Burian, taken in June 1995.*

ico is now back on course after being sidetracked in the colonial era. This sense of restored authority—reconstructed from a mythic past—is not exactly clear, but its implications are powerful.

For many readers in the United States, it is difficult to think about architecture in terms other than that of a utensil or an aesthetic commodity. In this sense, the depth of the conviction in the belief in modernity as an ideological enterprise in Mexico is startling. The "Janus-like" stance, as described by Antonio Méndez-Vigatá in his essay, of simultaneously invoking a mythic past and a utopian future, has been referred to by some authors as "time nostalgia." What is important to recognize in this double-faced operation is the repression of the present. By invoking another time, the complex reality of the present is de-emphasized.

Transition and dichotomy are themes that are seemingly embedded in this text. The dichotomy between the international avant-garde and the national and local is a theme that pervades many of the essays and appears in much of Latin American architecture, as well as art, literature, and music. Whether this opposition is endemic to the culture, or whether this is simply part of a transition to a homogeneous global culture, is an issue at the forefront of contemporary architectural practice in Mexico and the American Southwest.

Many of the architects discussed in this volume have been previously understood as transitional figures. Certainly Carlos Obregón Santacilia brings to mind architects such as George Howe in the United States who produced work in several architectural vocabularies. Juan Segura's innovative solutions to modern functional programs, while utilizing more traditional architectural vocabularies, recall Louis Sullivan's work. Juan O'Gorman, on the other hand, has never received his due attention among architectural historians, in part owing to the fact that his work was not a simple progression over a career. The relationship of O'Gorman to the Surrealist movement poses an interesting question that merits broader critical attention and may shed much light on his extraordinary work.

Much of the work discussed in the essays suggests the notion of *drift* across a career. Whether this phenomenon can be seen as the struggle between inherent dichotomies, as a more inclusive or pragmatic approach to alternative design vocabularies, or as the lack of a pervasive grounding in architectural theory is an interesting question to ponder.

Another approach to understanding the drift of a career is to recognize the historical context of knowledge. What we know and act upon stands on the shoulders of what precedes our current projects. In the case of the architect, past work becomes a historicist stepping stone. In this sense, what we build always modifies the meaning of what we built previously. Architects are both the receivers of the manifest meaning of their own works and the transformers of that meaning. No single work can be understood in isolation from its historical context or expressive drift.[1]

Ultimately, one of the most fundamental dichotomies raised is that between the technological *image* of a machine age and the handcrafted *reality* of Mexican production. This has resulted in a profound discontinuity of means and ends. As Alberto Pérez-Gómez has eloquently pointed out, the magical qualities of Mexican architecture come from "the love in a rough object that has little to do with clever, sophisticated theories," yet much to do with the earthbound tradition of *making* and the desire of the individual craftsperson to express and leave her or his mark on a place. In the current economic crisis, the material reality of architectural production will only make more visible the dichotomous condition of modernity in Mexico.

With the current tendency to reduce architecture to the mere manifestation of philosophical and literary texts, the refocusing of architecture as a physical presence seems all the more vital and important. In this regard, the material, physical-based reality of architecture, poetically felt and experienced by the human body, offers the possibility of a multitude of lessons about the making of architecture.

Edward R. Burian
Tucson, March 1995

Note

1. This insight was offered by Steven Moore, who pointed out that this position has previously been established by a number of writers including Theodor Adorno, Gianni Vattimo, and Richard Rorty, among others. For an examination of the relationship of works of architecture to their makers and receivers, see Steven Moore's unpublished doctoral dissertation, currently entitled "Building Soil and Architecture: Blueprint Demonstration Farm as a Case Study in Critical Regionalism."

NOTES ON THE CONTRIBUTORS

Alberto Pérez-Gómez is a native of Mexico City who is one of the leading architectural scholars in North America and Europe. He is currently the Saidye Rosner Bronfam Professor of the History of Architecture at McGill University, where he is Director of the program in the History and Theory of Architecture. He is also Director of the Institut de recherche en histoire de l'architecture, a research institute co-sponsored by the Canadian Centre for Architecture, the Université de Montreal, and McGill University. His book *Architecture and the Crisis of Modern Science* (MIT Press, 1983) won the Alice Davis Hitchcock Award in 1984—a prize awarded every two years for the most significant work of scholarship in the field—and has been translated into several languages. His latest book, *Polyphilo or the Dark Forest Revisited* (MIT Press, 1992), retells the love story of the famous Renaissance novel/treatise *Hypnerotomachia Poliphili* in late-twentieth-century terms. His essays have been published in numerous journals and periodicals, including *AA Files, Architecture Design, Arquitectura Bis, Arq, Harvard Architectural Review, Via,* and *Perspecta: The Yale Architecture Journal,* among others. He has also published two books of poetry in Spanish.

Antonio E. Méndez-Vigatá is the former Director of the Department of Architecture at the ITESM in Monterrey, Mexico, and has been a participant in numerous symposiums on Mexican architecture in North America. He has lectured in England, the United States, Spain, and Mexico. He has practiced architecture in Mexico since 1985 and currently practices in Torreón, where he recently completed an elementary school and a high school. He teaches at the Universidad Iberoamericana, Campus Laguna, in Torreón and also serves on the NAFTA commission that regulates architectural licensing between the United States and Mexico.

Celia Ester Arredondo Zambrano, a native of Monterrey, teaches architectural design, history, and theory at the ITESM in Monterrey, Mexico. She has published numerous articles on architecture in Mexico and has served as editor of the magazine *Arquitectura en el ITESM*. In addition to her academic career, she is also an urban designer in the city of Monterrey. She recently participated in the Plan Estratégico del Area Metropolitana de Monterrey 2020 (Strategic Plan for the Monterrey Metropolitan Area 2020).

Alberto Kalach is an emerging figure in contemporary architectural practice in Mexico. His work has been published in numerous books and periodicals, including *6 años de arquitectura en México 1988–1994* (UNAM, 1994), and exhibited in both the United States and Mexico. He currently teaches at the UNAM in Mexico City. A monograph on his architectural work is forthcoming from Rockport Publishers in the United States as part of a series on emerging architects around the world.

William J. R. Curtis is one of the leading architectural historians of his generation who has written extensively on various aspects of Modern architecture. His book *Modern Architecture Since 1900* (Phaidon, first edition, 1982; second edition, 1987; third edition, 1996) has received international recognition and has been translated into several languages. He is also the author of *Le Corbusier: Ideas and Forms* (Oxford, 1986), *Balkrishna Doshe: An Architecture for India* (Rizzoli, 1988), and *Denys Lasdun: Architecture, City, Landscape* (Phaidon, 1994). He has also written many essays on contemporary Spanish and Latin American architecture, including "Towards an Authentic Regionalism," *Mimar* 19, December 1985; "Mythical Landscapes, Modern Architecture and the Mexican Past," in *Hechos de Oaxaca* (Monterrey: MARCO, 1991); "Laberintos en temporales, Luis Barragán," in *Arquitectura y Vivienda* (Madrid, 1988; reprinted as an obituary for Luis Barragán in *Vuelta* in 1989); and "Modern Architecture and Mexican Conditions," in *Teodoro González de León: La voluntad de creador* (Bogotá: Escala-Somosur, 1994). Dr. Curtis has lectured and taught around the world and has held a number of honorary posts. He received the Alice Davis Hitchcock Medal of the Society of Architectural Historians in Great Britain in 1984; the Founders Award of the Society of Architectural Historians, U.S.A., 1982; Critics Award of the Comité International des Critiques d'Arquitectur in 1985; and a Silver Medal at the World Architectural Biennale in 1989.

Edward R. Burian, a native of Los Angeles, is a practicing architect based in Tucson, Arizona, whose writings and practice focus on the architecture and culture of the American Southwest and México. His architectural work has been published in both the United States and Mexico. He has taught in several schools of architecture in the Southwest, in the areas of architectural design and architectural history and theory, including seminars on the art and architecture of twentieth-century Mexico. An exhibition of his architectural projects, entitled "Edward R. Burian, Architect: Buildings and Projects for the American Southwest," will travel in the United States and Mexico. Currently, he is designing several residences in the Sonoran Desert in Tucson, Arizona.

Carlos G. Mijares Bracho is one of the leading practitioners in Mexico. His architectural work has been the subject of a monograph, *Carlos Mijares* (Bogotá: Editorial SomoSur, 1989). He was recently involved in the design of a major urban design intervention in Mexico City with an international cast of architects including Aldo Rossi, Fuhiko Maki, and Charles Correa, among others. He has taught at the Universidad Iberoamericana and the UNAM in Mexico City. His writings include "Arquitectura de nuestro tiempo," in *Cuarenta siglos de plástica mexicana* (Mexico: Editorial Herrero, 1971) as well as numerous articles on Mexican architecture. He recently participated in a symposium in Berlin with several other Mexican architects.

Antonio Toca Fernández has written many books and essays on Modern Mexican architecture. His books include *Juan Segura: Orígenes de la arquitectura moderna en México* (INBA, 1990); *Arquitectura posrevolucionaria en México* (INBA, 1962); *Arquitectura moderna en México 1900–1982* (UAM, 1989); and *México: Nueva arquitectura* (GG, 1991), with Aníbal Figueroa. He has won several awards for his work as a practicing architect, including the 3rd Biennele of Mexican Architecture for the Sinaloa Science Center and the Sinaloa Congress. He is currently Head of the Design Division of the IMMS in Mexico City.

Louise Noelle Merles is an architectural critic and historian whose writings focus on various aspects of Modern Mexican architecture. She is the author of several books and numerous articles, including *Agustín Hernández: Arquitectura y pensamiento* (UNAM, 1982; reprinted 1988); *Arquitectos contemporáneos de México* (Editorial Trillas, 1989; reprinted 1990); *Ricardo Legorreta, tradición y modernidad* (UNAM, 1989); *Guía de arquitectura contemporánea de la Ciudad de México* (Banamex, 1993); *Vladimir Kaspé, reflexión y compromiso* (Universidad La Salle, 1995); and *Luis Barragán, búsqueda y creatividad* (UNAM, 1996), among others. She has also given numerous courses and lectures in Mexican universities and international congresses. She was the editor of *Arquitectura/México* from 1976 to 1988, and since 1982 has been a researcher at the Instituto de Investigaciones

Estéticas (Institute of Aesthetics Research). She is involved in many organizations that support the study of architecture, including the Comité International des Critiques d'Architecture (CICA), of which she is a co-founder and served as Director, and the Mexican Association of Architectural Critics. She also serves on the boards of the Mexican Committee of Art Historians and the Commission for the Catalog of Mexican Contemporary Architecture. She has received numerous academic honors, including being named Honorary Academician of the Sociedad de Arquitectos Mexicanos (SAM; Mexican Society of Architects), and is a member of ICMOS Mexicano (International Council of Monuments and Sites for Mexico, under the auspices of UNESCO) as well as the Academia de Artes.

SELECTED BIBLIOGRAPHY

[*Note to the reader:* Although this book focuses on the time period from the end of the Mexican Revolution to the Olympic Games, I have also included reference material up to the present time because of the numerous overlaps which occur in terms of architects, buildings, and ideas, and the fact that much of this material is not well known to most English-speaking readers. Much of the early history of Modern architecture is featured in the periodicals of the time, which I have also listed. These include those published in Mexico as well as special issues published outside the country. Special thanks to Louise Noelle Merles and Antonio Toca Fernández for sharing their bibliographies on modern Mexican architecture.]

Abbreviations

CNAM	Colegio Nacional de Arquitectos de México
CNCA	Consejo Nacional de la Cultura y las Artes
IIE	Instituto de Investigaciones Estéticas (UNAM)
INAH	Instituto Nacional de Antropología e Historia
INBA	Instituto Nacional de Bellas Artes
SAIPN	Sociedad de Arquitectos del Instituto Politecénico
SAM	Sociedad de Arquitectos Mexicanos
SEP	Secretaría de Educación Pública
UAM	Universidad Autónoma Metropolitana
UAP	Universidad Autónoma Puebla
UNAM	Universidad Nacional Autónoma de México

Monographs on Individual Modern Mexican Architects and Buildings

Acevedo, J. *Disertaciones de un arquitecto.* Mexico City: Ediciones México Moderno, 1920; INBA, 1967, 1920.

Alvarez, A. *Augusto H. Alvarez, discurso, reflexión, ensayo, obras, curriculum.* Mexico City, 1984.

Amábilis, M. *El pabellón de México en la Exposición Iberoamericana de Sevilla.* Mexico City: Talleres Gráficos de la Nación, 1929.

Ambasz, E. *The Architecture of Luis Barragán.* New York: Museum of Modern Art, 1976.

Anda, E. X. de. *Luis Barragán: Clásico de silencio.* Colecciones SomoSur. Bogotá: Escala, 1989.

Artigas, F. *Francisco Artigas*. Mexico City: Editorial Tláloc, 1972.

Artigas, J. *Centro Cultural Universitario: Visita guiada en torno de su arquitectura*. Mexico City: UNAM, 1994.

———. *La Ciudad Universitaria de 1954: Un recorrido a cuarenta años de su inauguración*. Mexico City: UNAM, 1994.

Attoe, W. *The Architecture of Ricardo Legorreta*. Austin: University of Texas Press, 1990.

Auzelle, R. *Ramírez Vázquez*. Mexico City: Miguel Galas, 1989.

Barragán, Luis. *Luis Barragán, arquitecto*. Mexico City: Museo Rufino Tamayo, 1984.

Buschiazzo, M. F. *Félix Candela*. Buenos Aires: Instituto de Arte Americano, 1961.

Camberos Garibi, J. "Hannes Meyer: Su etapa en México." In *La arquitectura mexicana del siglo XX*. Ed. F. González Gortázar. Mexico City: Consejo Nacional para la Cultura y las Artes, 1994.

La Ciudad Iberoamericana. Valencia: Generalitat Valenciana, 1988.

La Ciudella-Biblioteca México. Mexico City: CNCA, 1991.

La construcción del Palacio de Bellas Artes. Documentos para la historia de la arquitectura mexicana, no. 1. Mexico City: INBA, 1984.

Faber, C. *Candela: The Shell Builder*. New York: Reinhold Publishing, 1963.

Ferrera, R. *Luis Barragán, capilla en Tlalpan*. Mexico City: Sirio Editores, 1980.

Figueroa, A. *El arte de ver con inocencia: Pláticas con Luis Barragán*. Mexico City: UNAM, 1989.

Garay, G. de. "La obra de Carlos Obregón Santacilia, arquitecto." *Cuadernos de Arquitectura y Conservación del Patrimonio Artístico* 6. Mexico City: INBA/SEP, 1979.

———, ed. "Augusto H. Alvarez." In *Historia oral de la ciudad de México: Testimonios de sus arquitectos, 1940–1990*. Mexico City: Instituto Mora, 1994.

García Oropeza, G., and A. Gómez Barbosa. *Luis Barragán*. Guadalajara: Universidad de Guadalajara, 1980.

Goeritz, M. "La integración plástica en el C.U. Presidente Juárez." N.p.

González de León, T., R. Legorreta, X. Moyssén, and L. Noelle. *Homenaje al arquitecto Mario Pani (1911–1993)*. Mexico City: Academia de Artes, 1993.

González Gortázar, F. *Conversaciones con Ignacio Díaz Morales sobre Luis Barragán.* Guadalajara: Universidad de Guadalajara, 1992.

——— *Mathías Goeritz en Guadalajara.* Guadalajara: Universidad de Guadalajara, 1991.

Heyer, P. *Abraham Zabludovsky, Architect.* New York: Princeton Architectural Press, 1993.

———. *Mexican Architecture: The Work of Abraham Zabludovsky and Teodoro González de León.* New York: Walker, 1978.

Iannini, H., comp. *Charlas de Pedro Ramírez Vázquez.* Mexico City: Ediciones Gernika-UAM, 1987.

Ideas y obras, Reynaldo Pérez Rayón. Mexico City: Edición del Arquitecto, 1990.

INBA/SEP. *4000 años de arquitectura en México.* Mexico City, 1963.

Jiménez, V., ed. *José Villagrán.* Mexico City: INBA, 1986.

Larrosa, M. *Mario Pani: Arquitecto de su época.* Mexico City: UNAM, 1985.

León, A. "Juan Segura." Professional thesis, Universidad Iberoamericana, Mexico City, 1982.

López Rangel, R. *Diego Rivera y la arquitectura mexicana.* México: SEP, 1986.

———. *Enrique Yáñez en la cultura arquitectónica mexicana.* Mexico City: Editorial LIMUSA-UAM, 1989.

Luis Barragán: Ensayos y apuntes para un bosquejo crítico. Mexico City: Museo Rufino Tamayo, 1985.

Luis Barragán Morfín, 1902–1988: Obra construída. Sevilla: Dirección General de Arquitectura y Vivienda, 1991.

Maya Gómez, I., and J. Torres Palacios. *La arquitectura de Manuel González Rul.* Mexico City, n.d.

———. *Manuel Rocha, en busca de una arquitectura mexicana.* Mexico City, c. 1979.

Noelle, L. *Agustín Hernández, arquitectura y pensamiento.* Mexico City: UNAM/IIE, 1982.

———. *Agustín Hernández, praxis y pensamiento, Mario Pani, respuesta.* Mexico City: Academia de Artes, 1993.

———. *Ricardo Legorreta, tradición y modernidad.* Mexico City: UNAM, 1989.

———. "Semblanza del arquitecto Enrique del Moral." In *Enrique del Moral: Imagen y obra escogida.* Colección México 64. Mexico City: UNAM, 1984.

———, ed. *Teodoro González de León: La voluntad del creador.* Colecciones SomoSur, no. 14. Bogotá: Escala, 1994.

O'Gorman, J. "El desarrollo de la arquitectura mexicana en los últimos treinta años." *Arquitectura* 23, 100 (April and June 1968).

Pani, M. *Los multifamiliares de pensiones.* Mexico City: Editorial Arquitectura, 1952.

————, and E. del Moral. *La construcción de la Ciudad Universitaria del Pedregal: Concepto, programa y planeación arquitectónica.* Mexico City: UNAM, 1979.

Pinoncelly, S. "Juan Segura, Precursor." *Excélsior* (Mexico City), November 21, 1965.

————. *La obra de Enrique del Moral.* Mexico City: UNAM, 1983.

Pizarro, J., ed. *Ramírez Vázquez.* Mexico City: Miguel Galas, 1989.

Rodríguez Prampolini, I. *Juan O'Gorman: Arquitecto y pintor.* Mexico City: UNAM, 1982.

————. *La palabra de Juan O'Gorman: Selección de textos.* Textos de humanidades, no. 37. Mexico City: UNAM/IIE, 1983.

Ruth Rivera, espacios de difusión arquitectónica. Mexico City: CNCA-SAIPN, 1989.

Saito, Yutaka. *Luis Barragán.* Tokyo, Japan: Toto Publishing, 1993.

Salas Portugal, A. *Barragán: Photographs of the Architecture of Luis Barragán.* New York: Rizzoli, 1992.

Santa María, R., and S. Palleroni. *Carlos Mijares: Tiempo y otras construcciones.* Colecciones SomoSur, no. 4. Bogotá: Escala, 1989.

Toca Fernández, A. *Juan Segura: Orígenes de la arquitectura.* Documentos para la Historia de la Arquitectura en México, no. 3. Mexico City: INBA, 1990.

Trueblood, B. *Ramírez Vázquez en la arquitectura: Realización y diseño.* Mexico City: Editorial Diana, c. 1989.

UNAM. *Pensamiento y destino de la Ciudad Universitaria de México: 1952.* Mexico City: Imprenta Universitaria, 1952.

Vago, P. *Pedro Ramírez Vázquez, un arquitecto mexicano.* Stuttgart, Germany: Karl Kramer, 1979.

Vargas Salguero, R. *José Villagrán.* Documentos para la historia de la arquitectura en México, no. 2. Mexico City: INBA, 1986.

————, ed. *Teoría de la arquitectura.* Mexico City: UNAM, 1988.

Villagrán García, J. *José Villagrán García: Imagen y obra escogida.* Mexico City: UNAM, 1986.

————. *Teoría de la arquitectura mexicana.* Mexico City: ASINEA, n.d.

———, ed. *Teoría de la arquitectura*. Mexico City: INBA/SEP, 1964.

Yáñez, E. *Arquitectura, teoría, diseño, contexto*. Mexico City: Limusa, 1982.

———. "Enrique Yáñez." *Arquitectura* 23, 100 (April and June 1968).

Modern Mexican Architecture: Surveys and Commentaries

Alva Martínez, E. *Jóvenes arquitectos mexicanos*. Mexico City: Comex, 1993.

Alva Martínez, E., and S. Schara. *Color en la arquitectura mexicana*. Mexico City: COMEX, 1992.

Anda, E. X. de. *La arquitectura de la Revolución Mexicana: Corrientes y estilos en la década de los veinte*. Mexico City: UNAM/IIE, 1990.

———. *Evolución de la arquitectura en México: Epocas prehispánica, virreinal, moderna y contemporánea*. Mexico City: Panorama Editorial, 1987.

Anuario de arquitectura mexicana. Mexico City: INBA, 1977.

Arquitectura contemporánea tapatía (catalog). Guadalajara: Academia de Arquitectura-Centro de Arte Moderno, 1993.

El Art-Decó en México. Mexico City: Instituto Mexicano–Norteamericano de relaciones culturales, 1977.

Bayón, D. *The Changing Shape of Latin American Architecture: Conversations with Ten Leading Architects*. New York: John Wiley, 1979.

Beacham, H. *The Architecture of Mexico; Yesterday and Today*. New York: Architectural Book Publishing, 1969.

Born, E. *The New Architecture in Mexico*. New York: W. Morrow, 1937.

Browne, E. *Otra arquitectura América Latina*. Mexico City: Gustavo Gili, 1988.

Bullrich, F. *New Directions in Latin American Architecture*. New York: George Braziller, 1969.

CAM. *Reseña de arquitectura mexicana/Mexican Architecture Review*. Mexico City: Editorial Enlace, 1992.

Camberos Garibi, J. *La arquitectura mexicana del siglo XX*. Mexico City: Consejo Nacional para la Cultura y las Artes, 1994.

———. *Cuarenta años de enseñanza universitaria de la arquitectura, 1948–1988*. Guadalajara: Universidad de Guadalajara, 1992.

Candela, F. *En defensa del Formalismo y otros escritos*. Madrid: Xarait Ediciones, 1985.

Catálogo de arquitectura mexicana contemporánea. Mexico City: CAM/SAM, 1994.

Cervantes, L. *Crónica arquitectónica prehispánica, colonial, contemporánea.* Mexico City: Editorial CIMSA, 1952.

Cetto, M. *Modern Architecture in Mexico.* New York: Praeger, 1961.

Curtis, W. "Laberintos intemporales." *Arquitectura y Vivienda* (August 1988).

Damaz, P. F. *Art in Latin American Architecture.* New York: Reinhold Publishing, 1963.

Espinosa, E. *L'Esprit Nouveau: Una estética moral purista y un materialismo romántico.* Mexico City: UNAM, 1986.

Espinoza López, E. *Ciudad de México, 1521–1980.* Mexico City: Edition of the author, 1991.

Esqueda, X. *Una puerta al Art-Deco.* Mexico City: UNAM, Centro de Investigación y Servicios Museográficos, 1980.

Fernández, J. *Arte moderno y contemporáneo de México.* Prologue by Manuel Toussaint. Mexico City: UNAM, 1952.

Glusberg, J. *Seis arquitectos mexicanos.* Buenos Aires: Ediciones de Arte Gaglianone, 1983.

Gómez, L., and M. A. Quevedo, eds. "Testimonios vivos: 20 arquitectos." *Cuadernos de Arquitectura y Conservación del Patrimonio Artístico* 15–16. Mexico City: INBA/SEP, 1981.

Gómez Mayorga, M. "La arquitectura contemporánea en México, notas polémicas." *Artes de México* 9, no. 36, 1961.

———. *Ensayos críticos sobre arquitectura.* Guadalajara: Universidad Autónoma de Guadalajara, 1977.

González Gortázar, F., ed. *La arquitectura mexicana del siglo XX.* Mexico City: Consejo Nacional para la Cultura y las Artes, 1994.

González Lobo, C. "La arquitectura mexicana en la cuarta década." *Cuadernos de Arquitectura y Conservación del Patrimonio Artístico* 22–23. Mexico City: INBA/SEP, 1982.

Grove, R. *Guía de arquitectura mexicana contemporánea.* Mexico City: Editorial Espacios, 1952.

Gutiérrez, R. *Arquitectura y urbanismo en Iberoamérica.* Madrid: Ediciones Cátedra, 1983.

Haas, A. *Jardines de México.* Mexico City: Lotería Nacional, 1993.

Hernández, A. *Gravedad, geometría y simbolismo.* Mexico City: UNAM, 1989.

Hernández, L. *Análisis crítico de la arquitectura moderna en*

México. Jalisco, Mex.: Escuela de arquitectura, Universidad de Guadalajara, 1965.

Hitchcock, H. R. *Latin American Architecture Since 1945.* New York: Museum of Modern Art, 1955.

INBA. *Arquitectura mexicana: 10 obras anuario: 1990.* Mexico City: INBA, n.d.

———. *El Museo Nacional de Arquitectura.* Mexico City: INBA, 1990.

INBA/SEP. "La práctica de la arquitectura y su enseñanza en México." *Cuadernos de Arquitectura y Conservación del Patrimonio Artístico* 26–27. Mexico City, 1983.

Islas, L. *Ciudad universitaria.* Colección Anáhuac de arte mexicano, no. 29. Mexico City: Ediciones de Arte, 1952.

Jiménez, V. "CAPFCE: 40 años de arquitectura." In *El Museo Nacional de Arquitectura.* Mexico City: INBA, 1990.

Kappe, S., ed. *Modern Architecture, Mexico.* Los Angeles, Calif.: Southern California Institute for Architecture, 1981.

Kaspé, V. *Arquitectura como un todo, aspectos teórico-prácticos.* Mexico City: Diana, 1986.

Katzman, I. *La arquitectura contemporánea mexicana: Precedentes y desarrollo.* Mexico City: INAH, 1963.

López Rangel, R. *Contribución a la visión crítica de la arquitectura.* Puebla: UAP, 1977.

———. *La modernidad arquitectónica mexicana: Antecedentes y vanguardias, 1900–1940.* Cuadernos temporales, no. 15. Mexico City: UAM, 1989.

———. *Orígenes de la arquitectura técnica en México.* Mexico City: UAM, 1984.

———, comp. *Las ciudades latinoamericanas.* Mexico City: Plaza y Valdez, 1989.

Manrique, J. A. *Proceso de las artes, 1910–1970.* Historia General de México, no. 4. Mexico City: El Colegio de México, 1977.

Mariscal, N. *La arquitectura en México.* Mexico City: Talleres Gráficos de la Nación, 1923.

Martín Hernández, V. *Arquitectura doméstica de la Ciudad de México, 1890–1925.* Mexico City: UNAM, 1981.

Maya Gómez, I., and J. Torres Palacios, eds. *Cuatro arquitectos mexicanos.* Mexico City: N.p., 1971.

Medel, V. *Diccionario de arquitectura mexicana.* Mexico City: Infoavit-Inbursa, 1994.

Melgar Adalid, M., and J. R. Alvarez Noguera. *Seis años de ar-*

quitectura en México, 1988–1994. Mexico City: UNAM, 1994.

Mijares, C. "Arquitectura de nuestro tiempo." In *Cuarenta siglos de plástica mexicana.* Mexico City: Editorial Herrero, 1971.

Moral, E. del. *El hombre y la arquitectura: Ensayos y testimonios.* Mexico City: UNAM, 1983.

Myers, I. E. *Mexico's Modern Architecture.* Prologue by Enrique Yáñez. New York: Architectural Book Publishing, 1952.

Neuvillate, A. de. *Diez arquitectos mexicanos.* Mexico City: Galería de Arte Misrachi, 1977.

Noelle, L. *Arquitectos contemporáneos de México.* Mexico City: Editorial Trillas, 1989.

———. *Crónicas de la Academia Nacional de Arquitectura.* Mexico City: UAM, 1992.

———. *El desarrollo urbano y Villahermosa.* Villahermosa, Mex.: Codeurtab, 1987.

———, and C. Tejeda. *Catálogo guía de arquitectura mexicana contemporánea, Ciudad de México.* Mexico City: Fomento Cultural Banamex AC, 1993.

Obregón Santacilia, C. *Cincuenta años de arquitectura mexicana (1900–1950).* Mexico City: Editorial Patria, 1952.

———. *Historia folletinesca del Hotel del Prado.* Mexico City: Imprenta Nuevo Mundo, 1951.

———. *El maquinismo, la vida y la arquitectura.* Mexico City: Publicaciones "Letras de México," 1939.

———. *Mexico como eje de las antiguas arquitecturas de América.* Mexico City: Editorial Atlante, 1947.

Olarte, L., S. Díaz, and J. Fernández. *Espacios, color y formas en la arquitectura: Guadalajara 1910–1942.* Guadalajara: Editorial Universidad de Guadalajara, 1990.

Pinoncelly, S. *La crítica de la arquitectura contemporánea.* Mexico City: n.p., 1964.

Quintero, P., comp. *Modernidad en la arquitectura mexicana: 18 protagonistas.* Mexico City: UAM, 1990.

Ricalde, H. *Arquitectura mexicana: 10 obras.* Houston: Wetmore, 1990.

Ríos González, E. "Crítica de ideas arquitectónicas." *Arquitectura* (June 1958).

Rossell, G. *Guía de la arquitectura mexicana contemporánea.* Mexico City: Editorial Espacios, 1952.

Sánchez de Carnona, M. *Catálogo de arquitectura mexicana, 1895–1991.* Mexico City: UAM, 1993.

Segre, R., and R. López Rangel. *Architettura e territorio nell'America latina.* Milan: Electa Editrice, c. 1982.

Segurajauregui, E. *Arquitectura porfirista: La Colonia Juárez*. Mexico City: UAM-Tilde, 1990.

Seminario La Posmodernidad (symposium). Mexico City: UAM, 1991.

Sigal, I. *Catálogo de publicaciones periódicas mexicanas de arquitectura, urbanismo y conexos. Cuadernos de Arquitectura y Conservación del Patrimonio Artístico 30–31*. Mexico City: INBA/SEP, 1985.

Smith, C. B. *Builders in the Sun: Five Mexican Architects*. New York: Architectural Book Publishing, 1967.

Sondereguer, P. C. *Memoria y utopía en la arquitectura mexicana*. UAM-Tilde, México, 1990.

Street-Porter, T. *Casa Mexicana: The Architecture, Design, and Style of Mexico*. New York: Stewart, Tabori and Chang, 1989.

Suzuki, M. "Modern Mexican Architecture." *Process Architecture* 39 (1983).

Tibol, R. *Epoca moderna y contemporánea*. Vol. 5–6 of *Historia general del arte mexicano*. Ed. P. Rojas. Mexico City: Editorial Hermes, 1963.

Toca Fernández, A. *Arquitectura contemporánea en México, 1900–1982*. Mexico City: UAM-Ediciones Gernika, c. 1989.

———. "Arquitectura posrevolucionaria en México." *Cuadernos de Arquitectura y Conservación del Patrimonio Artístico 20–21*. Mexico City: INBA/SEP, 1982.

———. *Más allá posmoderno*. Mexico City: Gustavo Gili, 1986.

———. *Mexico: Nueva arquitectura no. 2*. Mexico City: Ediciones Gustavo Gili, 1993.

———, and A. Figueroa. *México: Nueva arquitectura*. Mexico City: Ediciones Gustavo Gili, 1991.

Trueblood, B., ed. *Arquitectura de la ciudad de México*. Mexico City: N.p., 1976.

UNAM. *F. A. Documentos Vol. 1, 1986*. Mexico City: 1986.

Vargas Salguero, R. *La casa en el tiempo*. Mexico City: Calli no. 9, 1963.

———. *Historia de la teoría de la arquitectura: El porfirismo*. Mexico City: UAM, 1989.

Véjar Pérez-Rubio, C. *Crónicas y relatos de la arquitectura y la ciudad*. Mexico City: UAM-Ediciones Gernika, 1992.

Villagrán García, J. *Panorama de 50 años de arquitectura mexicana contemporánea*. Mexico City: INBA, 1952.

———. *Panorama de 62 años de arquitectura mexicana contemporánea. Cuadernos de Arquitectura y Conservación del Patrimonio Artístico 10*. Mexico City: INBA/SEP, 1963.

Yáñez, E. *Del funcionalismo al post-racionalismo.* Mexico City: UAM-Limusa, 1990.

———. *Dieciocho residencias de arquitectos mexicanos.* Mexico City: Ediciones Mexicanas, 1951.

———. *Hospitales de seguridad social.* 6th ed. Prologue by José Villagrán García. Mexico City: N.p., 1982.

Zambrano Villa, J. E. *Arquitectura para la educación superior.* Guadalajara: Universidad de Guadalajara, 1982.

Zevi, B. "Grottesco Messicano." *L'Espresso* (Rome), December 29, 1957.

General Histories of Mexico, Cultural Criticism, and General Reference

Adam, P. *Art of the Third Reich.* New York: Harry N. Abrams, 1992.

Althusser, L. "Ideology and Ideological State Apparatuses." In *Essays on Ideology.* London: Verso, 1984.

———. *La filosofía como arma de la revolución.* Mexico City: Siglo Ventiuno Editores, 1989.

Anderson, S. "The Fiction of Function." In *Putting Modernity in Its Place.* N.p., n.d.

Ashton, D. "Mexican Art of the Twentieth Century." In *Mexico: Splendors of Thirty Centuries.* New York: The Metropolitan Museum of Art, 1990.

Auerbach, E. *Mimesis: The Representation of Reality in Western Literature.* Princeton, N.J.: Princeton University Press, 1953.

Banham, R. *Theory and Design in the First Machine Age.* London: Architectural Press, 1960.

Bartra, R. *The Cage of Melancholy: Identity and Metamorphosis in the Mexican Character.* Trans. Christopher J. Hall, New Brunswick, N.J.: Rutgers University Press, 1992.

Benevolo, L. *Historia de la arquitectura moderna.* Barcelona: Gustavo Gili, 1982.

Borges, J. L. "Las ruinas circulares." In *Ficciones.* Buenos Aires: Emece Editores, 1956; Mexico City: Alianza Editorial, 1991.

Camp, R. A. *Intellectuals and the State in 20th-Century Mexico.* Austin: University of Texas Press, 1985.

Caso, A. *El problema de México y la ideología nacional.* Mexico City: Editorial Cultura, 1924.

Colomina, B., ed. *Sexuality and Space.* New York: Princeton Architectural Press, 1992.

Conrads, U., ed. *Programs and Manifestoes on 20th-Century Architecture.* Cambridge, Mass.: MIT Press, 1993.

Curtis, W. "Arquitectura moderna, condiciones mexicanas." In *Teodoro González de León: La voluntad del creador*. Ed. L. Noelle. Bogotá: Escala, 1994.

———. *Modern Architecture Since 1900*. London: Phaidon, 1982.

———. "Towards an Authentic Regionalism." *Mimar* 19 (December 1985).

Domenech, L. *Arquitectura de siempre: Los años 40 en España*. Barcelona: Tusquets, 1978.

Frampton, K. "Ten Points on an Architecture of Regionalism: A Provisional Polemic." *Center: A Journal for Architecture in America* 3 (1987).

———. "Toward a Critical Theory: Six Points for an Architecture of Resistance." In *The Anti-Aesthetic*. Ed. Hal Foster. Seattle: Bay Press, 1983.

Giedion, S. *Space, Time and Architecture: The Growth of a New Tradition*. Cambridge, Mass., and London: Harvard University Press, 1941.

Held, D. *Introduction to Critical Theory: Horkheimer to Habermas*. Berkeley: University of California Press, 1980.

Helm, M. *Modern Mexican Painters: Rivera, Orozco, Siqueiros and the Other Artists of the Social Realist School*. New York: Dover Publications, 1941.

Heyden, D., and P. Gendrop. *Pre-Columbian Architecture of Mesoamerica*. New York: Harry N. Abrams, 1975.

Hitchcock, H. R., and P. Johnson. *The International Style: Architecture Since 1922*. New York: W. W. Norton, 1932; 1966.

Kandell, J. *La Capital: The Biography of Mexico City*. New York: Random House, 1988.

Krauze, E. *Plutarco E. Calles*. Mexico City: Fondo de Cultura Económica, 1987.

Kubler, G. *The Shape of Time: Remarks on the History of Things*. New Haven: Yale University Press, 1962.

Lane, B. M. *Architecture and Politics in Germany, 1918–1945*. Cambridge, Mass.: Harvard University Press, 1968.

Le Corbusier. *The City of Tomorrow*. London: Architectural Press, 1978.

Loos, A. "Ornament and Crime." In *Programs and Manifestoes on 20th-Century Architecture*. Ed. U. Conrads. Cambridge, Mass.: MIT Press, 1970, 1993.

McHenry, J. P. *A Short History of Mexico*. Dolphin Books. Garden City, N.Y.: Doubleday, 1962.

Metropolitan Museum of Art. *Mexico: Splendors of Thirty Centuries*. New York: Bulfinch Press/Metropolitan Museum of Art, 1990.

Meyer, M. C., and W. L. Sherman. *The Course of Mexican History*. 3d ed. New York: Oxford University Press, 1987.

Miller, M. E. *The Art of Mesoamerica from Olmec to Aztec*. New York: Thames and Hudson, 1986.

O'Gorman, P. W. *Tradition of Craftsmanship in Mexican Homes*. Introduction by Juan O'Gorman. New York: Architectural Book Publishing, 1980.

Paz, O. *Essays on Mexican Art*. Trans. from the Spanish by Helen Lane. New York: Harcourt Brace Jovanovich, 1993.

———. *The Labyrinth of Solitude: Life and Thought in Mexico*. New York: Grove Press, 1962.

Pérez-Gómez, A. *Architecture and the Crisis of Modern Science*. Cambridge, Mass.: MIT Press, 1983.

———. "The Renovation of the Body: John Hejduk and the Cultural Relevance of Theoretical Projects." *AA Files* 13 (Autumn), 1986.

Piacentini, M. *Le Corbusier's "The Engineer's Aesthetic: Mass Production Houses."* (1922) Originally published in *Architettura e Arti Decorative II* (1922).

Polión, M. V. *Los diez libros de arquitectura*. Book 1, Chap. 3. Madrid: Ediciones Akal, 1991.

Puig Casauranc, J. M. *El sentido social del proceso histórico de México*. Mexico City: Ediciones Botas, 1936.

Reese, T. F., ed. *Studies in Ancient American and European Art: The Collected Essays of George Kubler*. New Haven: Yale University Press, 1985.

Riding, A. *Mexico: Inside the Volcano*. London: I. B. Taurus, 1987.

Romanell, P. *The Making of the Mexican Mind: A Study in Recent Mexican Thought*. Notre Dame, In.: University of Notre Dame Press, 1967.

Sáenz, M. *México íntegro*. Lima: Imprenta Torres Aguirre, 1929.

Schmidt, H. *The Roots of "Lo Mexicano": Self and Society in Mexican Thought, 1900–1934*. College Station, Tex.: Texas A&M University Press, 1978.

Scully, V. *American Architecture and Urbanism*. Rev. ed. New York: Henry Holt, 1988.

———. "Architecture: The Natural and the Manmade." In *Denatured Visions: Landscape and Culture in the Twentieth Century*. Ed. Stuart Wrede and William Howard Adams. New York: Museum of Modern Art, 1991.

SEP. *La educación pública en México.* Mexico City: Publicaciones de la Secretaría de Educación, 1926.

Smith, B. *Mexico: A History in Art.* Garden City, N.Y.: Gemini-Smith/Doubleday, 1968.

Smithsonian Institution Traveling Exhibition Service. *Mexico: A Landscape Revisited.* New York: Universe Publishing, 1994.

Speck, L. "Regionalism and Invention." *Center: A Journal for Architecture in America* 3 (1987).

Tafuri, M., and F. dal Co. *History of World Architecture I.* New York: Rizzoli, 1986.

———. *Modern Architecture.* New York: Harry N. Abrams, 1979.

Tegethoff, W. *Mies Van der Rohe: Villas and Country Houses.* New York: Museum of Modern Art, distributed by MIT Press, 1985.

Vasconcelos, José. *A Mexican Ulysses: An Autobiography.* Trans. and ab. by W. Rex Crawford. Part 3, "The Disaster." Bloomington, Ind.: Indiana University Press, 1963.

Periodicals

A&V. Madrid. No. 48, América Latina (1994).

Lo Actual en Arquitectura. Mexico City. Nos. 1–8, January 1993–1994.

Análisis Celular/Viviendas. Mexico City, UNAM. Nos. 1–10 (1978–1980).

Anuario de Arquitectura. In *Revista Arquitectura,* 1992–present. Mexico City.

El Arquitecto. Mexico City, SAM. (1923–1934).

Arquitectos de México. Mexico City. Nos. 1–24 (1960–1964).

Arquitectura de Yucatán, Cuadernos. Mérida, Facultad de Arquitectura-UADY. Nos.1–5 (1987–1992).

Arquitectura/México. Mexico City. Nos.1–119 (1938–1980) Special monographs in the following issues: No. 14, Iglesias; Nos. 15 and 103, Hospitales; No. 39, C.U.; No. 46, Acalpulco; No. 55, Villagrán; Nos. 61, 80, and 101, Guadalajara; No. 63, Escuelas; No. 84, Mercados; Anniversary Issue No. 83 and No. 100.

Arquitectura y Sociedad. Mexico City. Nos. 1–18 (1979–1985).

L'Arquitecture d'Aujord'hui. Paris. No. 58 (1955); No. 109 (1983), and No. 288 (1993).

Artes de México. Mexico City.

Calli. Mexico City. Nos. 1–65 (1960–1974).

Cemento. Mexico City. Nos. 1–38 (1925–1930).

Cuadernos de Arquitectura. Mexico City, INBA. Nos. 1–20

(1961–1966; including the following special issues: No. 10, Panorama de 52 años de arquitectura, by José Villagrán García; and No. 18, Nuevos ejemplos de arquitectura mexicana).

Cuadernos de Arquitectura Latinoamericana. UAP, Puebla, Nos. 1–3 (1977).

Cuadernos de Arquitectura y Conservación del Patrimonio Artístico. Mexico City, INBA/SEP. Nos. 1–31 (1979–1985; including No. 3, Una década de arquitectura mexicana; and Nos. 20–21 and 22–23, Apuntes para la historia y crítica de la arquitectura mexicana del siglo XX).

Enlace. Mexico City. August 1991–January 1995.

Espacios. Mexico City. Nos. 1–43 (1948–1959).

Etorno. Mexico City. Nos. 1–8 (1982–1984).

Etorno Inmobiliario. Mexico City. Nos. 1–12 (December 1992–December 1994).

Memoria de Papel. Mexico City: CNCA. No. 6 (June 1993).

Obras. Mexico City (January 1973–January 1993).

Revista Arquitectura. Mexico City. No. 1 (May 1991 to present).

Sumarios. Buenos Aires. Vol. 7, no. 34 (1980).

Techniques et Architecture. Paris. No. 320 (1978).

Traza. Mexico City. Nos. 1–10 (1983–1985).

Universidad de México. Mexico City. Ciudad Universitaria, Special issue (1994).

INDEX

Boldfaced page numbers indicate illustrations.

abstraction, 118

Aburto, Alvaro, 63, 173

Academy of San Carlos, 16, 75, 77, 152, 165

Administrative Committee for the Federal School Construction Program (CAPFCE), 82

Alemán, Miguel (President), 83

Althusser, Louis, 64

Alvarez, Augusto, 5, 79

Alvarez Espinosa, Roberto: Department of Medicine at Ciudad Universitaria, 99

Amábilis, Manuel, 72–74; Mexico Pavilion at the IberoAmerican Exhibition, 74

Anderson, Stanford, 132

Aragón Echeagaray, Enrique, 4; arcade in Mexico Park, 68,

architectural historians: in Mexico, 9

architectural practice in post-Revolutionary Mexico: background of, 165–166, 178; drift across a career, 193; perception of architects in, 165

architecture in relationship to the body, 194

Arquitectura/México, 188

Art Deco: ambiguity of, in Mexico, 173–174; and the work of Juan Segura, 172–174; in Mexico, 154–155, 159

Art Nouveau, 173–174

Associated Civil Engineers (ICA), 180

Auerbach, Erich, 71

Avila Camacho, Manuel (President), 81–83

Bachini, Angel, 72

Banham, Reyner, 132

Barragán, Luis, 4, 10, 45, 117, 119, 173; architect's own residence, 123; Gardens of Pedregal, 108–109, 192; house for two families on Avenida Parque, 192; in relationship to modernity, 14–15

Barreda, 21–22

Bartra, Roger, 70, 85, 93

Bauhaus, 102, 186

Beaux Arts influence: in Europe, 174; in Mexico, 22, 33, 152, 166, 174; in the work of Mario Pani, 177–178; in the writing of Villagrán, 38, 77

Boari, Adamo, 72

Borges, Jorge Luis, 91, 105

Born, Esther: influence of writings of, 7, 174

Bravo, Jorge: Olympic Stadium at Ciudad Universitaria, 107, 108, 109–110, 111, 112, 113

Breton, André, 35

Cacho, Raúl, 79; auditorium, Science Complex at Ciudad Universitaria, 102

Campos, Mauricio, 82

Campuzano, Jorge: Museo Nacional de Antropología e Historia, 41–42, 42, 59

Candela, Félix, 46–47; Church of

St. Joseph the Worker, 48; Cosmic Ray Lab at Ciudad Universitaria, 101, 104
CAPFCE (Administrative Committee for the Federal School Construction Program), 82
Cárdenas, Lázaro (President), 78–81
Caso, Antonio, 24, 86
Cavallari, Javier: Academy of San Carlos, 16
Cetto, Max, 4, 127
Chávez, Carlos, 71
Ciudad Universitaria (CU), 40, 83, 91–106, 157; *frontones*, 103; Main Library, 96–97; relationship to pre-Hispanic planning, 96, 109; Rectors Tower, 25, 85, 96, 187; School of Medicine, 99; School of Science, 97; site planning, 95–103; stadium, 103, 107, 107–114, 108, 111, 112, 113
Cloquet, Luis, 152
Colomina, Beatriz, 139
Colosio, Luis, 191
Comte, Auguste, 21–22; influence on Barreda, 21; in relationship to Beaux Arts instrumentality, 22; the engineer as the new aristocrat, 22; influence on Mexican Positivism. *See also* Díaz, Porfirio; Positivism
craft and materials, 30–31, 41, 45, 120–123, 147; in the work of Juan O'Gorman, 137–139, 141; in the work of Juan Segura, 170. *See also* tectonics
Cristeros movement, 72
critical regionalism, 42; as a devalued concept, 118; and the Modern movement in general, 115
CU. *See* Ciudad Universitaria
Cubism: and Luis Barragán's own

house, 123; and the development of Modern Mexican architecture, 31–32
Cuevas, José Luis, 82, 188
Cuicuilco, 94

de Jesús Lima, José, 179
de la Lama, Victor, 5
de la Mora y Palomar, Enrique, 4, 6, 10, 46–47; apartment building on Calle Strasburgo, 23; Church of St. Joseph the Worker, 48
Del Moral, Enrique, 4, 166, 173; architect's own house in Tacubaya, 115–126, 116, 120, 121, 122, 124; background, 118–119; Children's Home School, 76, 79; Mercardo de la Merced, 119; Ministry of Hydraulic Resources, 187; office building (corner of Insurgentes and Londres), 5; Plaza de Toros in Acapulco, 187; primary school in Casacuarán, 119; primary school in Yuriria, 82; Rector's Tower at Ciudad Universitaria 25; site plan for Ciudad Universitaria, 92, 95
Díaz, Porfirio (President), 21–22, 130, 163, 172. *See also* Comte, Auguste; Positivism
Díaz Morales, Ignacio, 4, 146
Durand, J. N. L., 15, 77

École de Beaux Arts. *See* Beaux Arts influence
education: Ministry of, 63–64, 71–72, 81; role of, in post-Revolutionary governments, 65–66
Elías Calles, Plutarco (President), 71–75
ensemble, 165
Escobedo, Helen: *Space* environ-

mental sculpture, 55
Exposition of Decorative Arts in
    Paris in 1925, 173–174

Felegruez, Manuel: *Space* environ-
    mental sculpture, 55
Frampton, Kenneth, 42
French culture: influence in Mexico,
    159
Functionalism, 28, 33, 77; ambigu-
    ity of, 132, 133; conceived in
    relationship to nationalism,
    101; diverse variants of,
    173–174; in Obregón Santa-
    cillia's work, 155; in O'Gor-
    man's work, 128, 132; origins
    of, 34; in the work of Mario
    Pani, 186

García Ramos, Domingo, 188
Garnier, Tony, 174
gesamtkunstwerk, 102
Giedeon, Sigfried, 117
Goeritz, Mathías: *Space* environ-
    mental sculpture, 55
González de León, Teodoro, 4, 108
González Reyna, Jorge, 5, 9; Cos-
    mic Ray Laboratory at Ciudad
    Universitaria, 101, 104
Gorbea Trueba, José, 4
Greenham, Carlos, 81; Main Hos-
    pital of the National Railroads
    of Mexico, 80
Gropius, Walter, 101, 117, 173
Guadalajara School, 146
Guadet, Julien, 15, 16, 77, 152
Guerrero, Enrique: School of
    Chemical Sciences at Ciudad
    Universitaria, 100

Hejduk, John, 59–60
Hernández, Agustín, 4
Hersua: *Space* environmental sculp-
    ture, 55

Hildalgo, Miguel: Jesuit education
    of, 18
Hoffman, Josef, 174
Howe, George, 193

ICA (Associated Civil Engineers),
    180
IMMS (Mexican Social Security
    Institute), 81
Institutional Revolutionary Party
    (PRI), 62, 191
instrumentality, 22–23
integración plastica, 83, 157, 184
International Style, 74–75, 98, 103,
    108, 115, 141, 144; critique of,
    in Mexico, 175
Italian fascism: and Mexican archi-
    tecture, 159
Izquierdo, María, 146

Jesuits: influence on modern
    thought in Mexico, 19–21. *See
    also* Villapando, Juan Batista

Kahlo, Frida: studio by Juan
    O'Gorman, 137–140
Kaspé, Vladimir, 5, 6, 9; Escuela
    Albert Einstein, 83; Humanities
    Building at Ciudad Universi-
    taria, 98, 100
Kubler, George, 146

Landa, Enrique, 5
Lazo, Carlos, 94, 103
League of Revolutionary Writers
    and Artists, 78
Le Corbusier, 27; influence on
    Mario Pani, 182; influence on
    Mural movement in Mexico,
    186; influence of theory in Mex-
    ico, 33, 36, 47–48, 77, 100,
    119, 129, 168, 173; window
    wall as camera lens, 139
Legarreta, Juan, 4, 9, 63, 130,

173, 175. *See also* Polytechnic
School of Architecture
Legorreta, Ricardo, 4, 146
Lelo, Luis, 83
Lloyd Wright, Frank, 36, 115, 143,
159
López García, Francisco: office
building (corner of Insurgentes
and Londres), 5

Marxism, 30
Mendelsohn, Erich, 159
Mendiola, Vicente, 4, 166
Mérida, Carlos, 183; *Juego de
Niños*, 183
mestizaje, 83–84, 147
mexicanidad, 70, 84, 133
Mexican Mural movement, 27–29,
31–32
Mexican Social Security Institute
(IMMS), 81
Mexico City: quality of life, 58–60
Meyer, Hannes, 6, 9; CAPFCE, 82;
Hospital Planning Commission,
82; role at the Polytechnic,
26–27, 46
Mier and Pesado Foundation, 166,
172
Mijares Bracho, Carlos G., 4
Mijares, Rafael: Museo Nacional
de Antropología e Historia,
41–42, 42, 59
Modern Mexican architecture: and
the avant-garde, 50;
dichotomies of, 193; and history of Modern architecture and
the acquisition of knowledge,
115–118, 174, 193–194; and
industrialization and prefabrication, 45; portrayal in books in
English, 7; portrayal in books in
Spanish, 7; in relationship to
literary theory and magical realism, 50–51; in relationship to
nationalism, 44; in relationship
to postmodernity, 51–53,
56–57; in relationship to pre-
Columbian architecture, 40,
42–43, 134; in relationship to
the pre-Columbian past, 192;
support for the study of, in
Mexico, 9; transitions in, 193;
youthfulness of major protagonists of, 84
Moderne, 173
Modernism: changing agendas,
119; in Mexico, 34–35
modernity: as an autonomous aesthetic practice, 191; challenges
to, in Mexico, 191; and concept
of a new universal man, 91–93,
104–105; and economic and
ecological realities in Mexico,
181; end of, in Mexico, 191;
ideological implications, 14,
118, 192–193; and material
implications of architectural
production, 191; in Mexico in
relationship to Europe, 15, 16
Montenegro, Roberto, 67; arcade
in Mexico Park, 68
multifamiliares, 180
Muñoz, García, Antonio: Central
Primary School of the Revolution, 78

NAFTA (North American Free
Trade Agreement), 3
National Academy of Architecture,
188
National University School of Ar-
chitecture, 37, 76; Mario Pani
at, 177, 188
nationalism, 93, 101, 103, 115
Neoclassicism in Mexico, 16
Neo-Colonial movement, 61, 66–70

Neopre-Hispanic revival, 72–74

North American Free Trade Agreement (NAFTA), 3

Obregón, Alvaro, President, 67, 154

Obregón, José, 43

Obregón Santacila, Carlos, 4, 67, 151–161, 166, 173, 193; background, 151–152; Bank of Mexico, 154; Cine Coliseo, 155; decline of productivity, 160; Department of the Federal district, 154; Escuela Benito Juárez 67, 70, 124, 166; Guardiola Building, 156, 156–157; Hotel del Prado, 156–157; Hotel Reforma, 156; IMSS Building, 81, 158; individual buildings in relationship to urban design, 156–157; Lachica Residence, 155; Ministry of Foreign Relations Building, 154; Ministry of Health and Assistance, 152, 153, 154, 157, 159; Monument for Cuauhtémoc, 154; Monument to the Revolution, 155, 156–157; Morin Residence, 154; painting and sculpture in his buildings, 157; Pani Residence, 155; Pavilion at the Rio de Janeiro Exhibition, 67, 154; Pension Administration Building, 156; Santacilia Building, 154; School for the Blind and Mute, 74, 154; Seguros de Mexico Building, 155; Social Security Building, 156–157

O'Gorman, Juan, 4, 10, 63, 98, 101, 173; Anhuacalli Project for Diego Rivera, 141; anthropomorphic relationships, 147; background, 129; Central Library at the Ciudad Universitaria, 140, 142; C.T.M. Project, 79; dichotomies in the work of, 128–129; house for Dr. Luis Erro, 133–134, 134; Kahlo/Rivera Studios, 136, 138, 138–140; Lerma Waterworks, 141; manifestos, 36, 133; masks in the work of, 142–143; organic architecture, 133; overview of his career, 127–149; as a painter, 140; Pedregal Residence, 143, 144, 145; and the Polytechnic School of Architecture, 26; Preliminary Scheme for Federal District Workers Housing, 79, 131; primary schools and his relationship to Narciso Bassols, 77–78, 130; studio and apartment for Frances Toor, 135, 135–137; and the Surrealist movement, 193; Taxco Mural Project, 141; The City of Mexico, 140, 141; The Myths, 140; Vocational School, 79.

Olbrich, Joseph Maria, 174

Olympic Games in Mexico (1968), 50

Orozco, José Clemente, 72, 83, 163, 178; La primavera, 182

Ortega Flores, Salvador: Rectors Tower at Ciudad Universitaria, 25

Ortega y Gasset, José, 30

Ortiz, Enrique: office building (corner of Insurgentes and Londres), 5

Ortiz Monasterio, Luis, 178

Ortiz Monasterio, Manuel, 4; The National Insurance Company Building, 5

Oud, Jacobus Johannes Pieter, 159

Pani, Mario, 5, 177–189; back-

ground, 177–179;
condominiums: Condominium
Law, 186; Condominium Los
Cocos, 186
hospitals: National Hospital Plan,
178; National Medical Center,
178; for tuberculosis in Perote,
178; for tuberculosis in Saltillo,
178; for tuberculosis in Tulancingo, 178
hotels: Hotel Alameda, 178; interventions in the Hotel del Prado,
156; Hotel Plaza, 178; Hotel
Reforma, 178
master plan projects, 188; for the
Ciudad Satellite, 188; for the
Ciudad Universitaria, 92, 95,
187–188. *See also* Ciudad Universitaria
miscellaneous projects: Ministry
of Hydraulic Resources, 187;
Plaza de Toros in Acapulco, 187
multifamily housing projects,
49–50, 87; Alemán Urban
Housing Project, 179–182, 180,
181; Juárez Urban Housing Project, 182–186; 183, 184, 185;
Multifamily Housing for University Faculty, 186; Nonoalco-
Tlatelolco Urban Housing
Project, 35, 186, 187; Santa Fe
Housing Project of the Mexican
Social Security Institute, 186
schools: National Music Conservatory, 83, 178, 179; National
Teachers College, 83, 178; Rector's Tower, 25; Teacher's
School, 83
Partido Socilista del Sureste, 72
patio: as a type, 119
Paz, Octavio, 14, 15, 30, 56–57,
62–63, 84

Pérez Palacios, Augusto, 5;
Olympic Stadium at the Ciudad
Universitaria, 107, 108, 109–
110, 111, 112, 113
Pérez Rayón, Reinaldo, 46
Perrault, Charles, 38
Perret, Auguste, 174
Peschard, Eugenio: auditorium,
Science Complex at Ciudad
Universitaria, 102
politics: and architectural language,
61–89
Polytechnic School of Architecture,
26; curriculum in relationship
to the National University, 26;
founding by Juan Legarreta and
Juan O'Gorman, 130
Positivism, 21–22, 130. *See also*
Comte, Auguste; Díaz, Porfirio
PRI (Institutional Revolutionary
Party), 62, 191

Quezada, Armando, 178
Quintana, Bernardo, 180

Ramírez Vázquez, Pedro, 4, 50,
109; critique of Ciudad Universitaria, 96, 103; Department of
Medicine at Ciudad Universitaria, 99; Ministry of Foreign
Relations, Plaza of the Three
Cultures, 28; Museo Nacional
de Antropología e Historia,
41–42, 42, 59; rural schools,
82–83
Reynaud, 77
Rivera, Diego, 28, 67, 70, 72, 78,
110, 114, 163; stained glass
windows in Ministry of Health
Building, 159; studio by Juan
O'Gorman, 137–140; *The Exploited Mexican People*, 73; *The*

Legacy of Independence, 20;
  The Painter's Studio, 139
Rivera, Ruth, 29, 32
Rossell, Guillermo: School of
  Chemical Sciences at Ciudad
  Universitaria, 100
Ruiz Massieu, Francisco, 191

Salas Portugal, Armando, 108–109
Salinas, Raul: Olympic Stadium at
  Ciudad Universitaria, 107, 108,
  109–110, 111, 112, 113
Sánchez Baylon, Félix: auditorium,
  Science Complex at the Ciudad
  Universitaria, 102
Schindler, Rudolf, 117
Scully, Vincent, 144
Sebastián: *Space* environmental
  sculpture, 55
Segura, Juan, 4, 163–176, 193;
  background, 163–165; design of
  ornament, 170–171; efficient
  utilization of resources, 172;
  Elderly Care Facility in Orizaba,
  170; Ermita Building, 164,
  165–168, 167, 168, 169, 170;
  Eugenia Building, 170; Isabel
  Building, 170, 171; new archi-
  tectural programs of, 166; work
  of, and urban design, 164
separation of church and state,
  65–66
Serrano, Francisco, 4, 173; Cine
  Encanto, 6
Silva, Fredrico: *Space* environmental sculpture, 55
Siqueiros, David Alfaro, 28–29, 72,
  163
Socialist Architects Union, 78
Sordo Madaleno, Juan, 5; Anahuac
  Insurance Building, 5
Sullivan, Louis, 193

Surrealism, 137, 147
symbolic order, 31, 48–49

Taller de Urbanismo, 188
Tamayo, Rufino, 54–55, 146
Tarditi, Carlos, 166, 173, 175;
  monument for Cuauhtémoc,
  154
technocracy, 37, 54
technology, 37, 46–47, 56, 119;
  and O'Gorman's views on architecture, 131–132, 170; in relationship to the discontinuity of
  means and ends, 194; and the
  work of Juan Segura, 164–165
tectonics, 110; in relationship to
  handcraft production, 194; in
  the Kahlo/Rivera studios of
  O'Gorman, 137–138; in relationship to materials and systems of production, 192; in the
  work of Juan Segura, 164. *See
  also* craft and materials
tepetate, 110
Tolsá, Manuel: Hospicio Cabañas,
  16, 18
Torres, Ramón, 5; Department of
  Medicine at Ciudad Universitaria, 99

unidad habitational, 183
Universidad Anáhuac, 188

van der Rohe, Mies, 45, 173; as
  catalyst for del Moral and Barragán, 123–125
Vasconcelos, José, 24–25, 30,
  66–67, 154, 165–166
Velázquez, Héctor, 5; Department
  of Medicine at the Ciudad Universitaria, 99
Vignola, Giacomo da, 16

Villagrán García, José, 4, 119, 146,
166, 173; Children's Home
School, 76, 79; Children's Hospital, 79; Department of the
Federal District, 154; Escuela
Rancho del Rosario, 82; Estadio
Nacional, 67–70, 69, 166;
Granja Sanitaria, 74; Huipulco
Tuberculosis Sanitarium, 76, 77;
in relationship to Le Corbusier,
40; National Cardiology Insti-
tute, 79, 79; National Medical
Center, 178; omission of pre-
Enlightenment theory in his
writings, 15; República de
Costa Rica School, 82; School
at Colonia Garza, 82; *Teoría de
la Arquitectura* in relationship
to Vitruvius and Perrault 37–38;
theories and writings of, 15, 37,
76–77, 178; Villagrán García
residence, 6
Villapando, Juan Bautista, 18, 20;
and relationship of Temple of
Solomon to the Cathedral in
Mexico City, 18–19. *See also*
Jesuits
Viollet-le-Duc, Eugéne-Emmanuel,
47
Vitruvius, 37–38, 77, 98

Wagner, Otto, 159, 174
women: role in modern architecture
in Mexico, 9

Xitle, 108, 114

Yale University, 37, 53
Yáñez, Enrique, 5, 79, 173, 175;
Hospital de la Raza, 82, 98;
School of Chemical Sciences at
Ciudad Universitaria, 100;
Teacher's School, 83

Zabludovsky, Abraham, 4
Zedillo, Ernesto (President), 191
zeitgeist, 117
Zohn, Alejandro: Sports Complex,
47

Milton Keynes UK
Ingram Content Group UK Ltd.
UKHW021524120924
448236UK00004B/80

9 780292 708532